I Left My Heart in Shanghi, Alabama

Also by Carroll Dale Short

The Shining Shining Path (novel), 1995

A Migration of Clowns (poems and essays), 2000

A Writer's Tool Kit (textbook), 2001

Turbo's Very Life and Other Stories (short fiction), 2006

In Search of the Spirit: Some Thoughts on Faith (essays), 2012

I LEFT MY HEART IN SHANGHI, ALABAMA

Essays on Home and Place

CARROLL DALE SHORT

NEWSOUTH BOOKS
Montgomery

NewSouth Books
105 S. Court Street
Montgomery, AL 36104

Published in the United States by NewSouth Books, a division of NewSouth, Inc., Montgomery, Alabama.

ISBN 978-1-60306-207-7 (pbk)
ISBN 978-1-60306-208-4 (ebk)

An earlier version of this book was published in 1988 by Media Shop Books without an ISBN. Unless otherwise noted, all the essays were first published in the *Daily Mountain Eagle* of Jasper, Alabama. The profiles in "Two Musicians" first appeared in *Birmingham Magazine*, and "A Thanksgiving Memory" first appeared in the *Birmingham News*.

Design by Randall Williams

Printed in the United States of America

For all my kin:
past, present, and future;
and with appreciation to Woni Lawrence,
reader and bookseller extraordinaire,
for invaluable help with manuscript preparation

Contents

Introduction to the 2012 Edition

I put off going home as long as I could, because home is gone. Or at least my family's portion of it is—the jagged swath of land and houses cut into hilly, coal-mining country roughly midway between Birmingham and Jasper, Alabama. Five generations of us called it home for more than a hundred years, watching for the community's soldiers to come home from World War I in the same front yards where we would later peer into a K-Mart telescope late at night to catch a glimpse of the U.S. space shuttle in low earth orbit.

I don't remember a time when any of us ever thought the place would last. Jesus was always just on the verge of coming back to earth, and my most recurring nightmare was the godawful mess that the Book of Revelation's beasts and giant white horses would make of my grandmother's flower garden in the process.

During my teenage years it appeared that global nuclear war might beat Jesus to the punch. And even after the Cuban Missile Crisis settled down, the usual threatening fare rumbled constantly at our perimeters: dynamite blasts from strip mines, tornadoes remaking the texture of the landscape even more summarily than land developers could.

Nobody ever anticipated that the end would come in a simple letter from the state highway department.

As it turned out, the Appalachian Development Highway System—a federal ball set rolling in 1963 by President John F. Kennedy—had finally worked its way down through geographical latitudes and letters of the alphabet to a massive project with the working name "Corridor X," a long overdue interstate that would mainly bear commercial truck traffic between Birmingham and Memphis, which was once recognized as the most heavily traveled highway of its length in the U.S.

Then we heard that the Corridor would miss Shanghi by a stone's throw. Doomsday had been a false alarm. But as the sight of surveying crews at the edge of town became more and more common, we realized something was up. The false-alarm news had itself been false, and the process of eminent domain was now taking a portion of Shanghi for use as a cloverleaf ramp.

One day I mentioned this fact to a magazine editor for whom I'd written articles in the past. He asked if I'd be interested in writing a piece about the demise of our homeplace, and I agreed.

In the coming weeks, as I did my research, I started by going to the scene of the crime: the Highway Department offices where administrators and engineers had initially sketched out the route of the new Corridor. Seen in isolation in their bright fluorescent offices, the progression of maps looked neat, professional, reasonable.

I was introduced to a gentleman who worked as "community liaison" for the department, a euphemism for the thankless job of standing in front of a succession of auditoriums and explaining to angry residents why their peaceful town was about to be split by an interstate.

I found him disturbingly likeable. He told me he had mostly learned to take the resultant hard feelings from his job in stride, and that he'd probably react the same way if his own homeplace was threatened. He also said the public forums he spoke to were remarkably similar:

"At some point, a person in the audience will stand up and say, 'The whole reason I moved out here was to get away from six-lane highways!' And I have to say, 'Yes ma'am, but if so many of y'all hadn't moved out here, we wouldn't need to *build* a six-lane highway."

At the end of my conversation with the Highway Department guy, as we were shaking hands goodbye, he said as an afterthought: "You know, the name of your road didn't help matters any." I must have looked blank because he prompted me, "Corridor X?" Indeed, the temporary name of the interstate had seemed to add insult to injury. "Had a science-fiction sound," he said. "Like 'X, the unknown.' I even had one man tell me it was part of a secret government plot."

We laughed at this. "I showed him on a map where Corridor W and Corridor Y were being built," he said. "But I don't think he believed me."

My journalistic research even included an evening at an ancient drive-in theater advertising a showing of "Twister," the unspoken moral of whose airborne, terrified heifers was that my hometown could have fared a lot worse.

I finished my magazine article on deadline, submitted it, and a few days later got a call from the editor, who sounded nervous. He said he was disappointed but they'd have to pay me a "kill fee"—a polite term in the publishing industry for a token payment to help cover expenses when a manuscript is deemed not suitable for print.

He apologized again and again, saying that, compared to my other writing he'd used in the past, the Shanghi piece was "oddly passionless."

And he was right.

On a cloudy spring morning in 2012, my longtime friend Rick Watson and I are poking through a dense patch of vines and brush in some woods near a highway cloverleaf of Highway I-22 where, as near as we can tell, my childhood home once stood.

It occurs to me that this is how a professional archaeologist must feel, silently combing through a mute section of landscape—attention focused on pursuit of even the smallest clue that might surface and suggest some recognizable plan or purpose of earlier human beings who have long since rotted and turned to dirt. Except that in this case I could be nowhere near objective because their whole purpose was myself, and their plan was to get me through the first twenty years of my life.

Eerily, nothing in the landscape seems at all familiar to me. The breeze on our faces quickly becomes cooler, and the slightest mist of rain begins. Then we half-heartedly pull apart a tangle of kudzu, and the corner of a grayed concrete slab appears. We stomp on the low brush and find that the concrete extends a few yards in both directions. A small light bulb flicks on in my memory: the rectangular surface must be the small square patio my grandfather built for us in the sloping side yard—a square concrete picnic table around a broad old oak, and just enough room at its perimeter to set up a barbecue grill and some folding lawn chairs, for occasions such as the Fourth of July and Labor Day.

If that's the case, then the ruin of the main house will be about fifteen long strides directly through the more dense brambles to the southwest. But even the hoe that Rick has brought allows us to chop only so far into the dark damp greenery and we can see no chunk of remaining structure larger than a pair of old mortar-joined concrete blocks.

But we tramp onward, and eventually my shoe hits an unseen chunk that sounds like glass: what we dig up is an empty, half-buried Pepsi-Cola bottle. Eureka; a sign of life. Then another bottle, and another, and then a king-sized ginger ale.

A few more yards of the hoe doubling as a swing-blade, and it hits a different kind of glass: brown-colored, with a much more solid sound. The engraving on the glass informs us, "Pabst Blue Ribbon." As I'm examining the bottle Rick comments, "We're drifting too far from the shore."

I break out laughing and can't stop, because we both know the old gospel hymn by heart in its entirety, even the little harmony runs done in an ethereal tenor, echoing "Peaceful shore...peaceful shore..." and we both know that my grandparents, after finding Jesus, had never let any form of alcohol cross their lips again.

At that point I'm holding a muddy Pepsi bottle in one hand and a muddy Pabst in the other, and as I go to toss them into the back of his pickup truck as souvenirs the rain shower increases in strength until it's impossible to see across the old road; the individual pines become just a blur of gray and green.

That's the moment I stub my toe on a rusty, half-buried cooking pot.

These days, the way you get to Shanghi, Alabama, is to start by spelling it wrong. Every navigational device I've found spells the community "Shanghai" and shows as its central feature Shanghai Memorial Cemetery, which in a way is true. Though alongside the large and perfectly-kept graveyard sits the same small, white-clapboard Shanghi Baptist Church that generations of my family attended, and on a pew of which my great-grandfather John Brasfield died of a heart attack during a Sunday evening service. He passed so silently and without warning that his family assumed, until church was over, that he had only dozed off.

Nowadays, to drive to Shanghi from the county seat of Jasper you head east on the former Corridor X, whose signs now say Interstate 22. After about 16 miles you take Exit 78 and bear right onto County Road 81, a two-lane blacktop surrounded on both sides by woods. About a third of a mile later, a random grove of mimosas appears on the right, offspring of the ones my grandmother imported into her yard over the years because she liked the pink color of the blossoms and the fact that the structure of each one looked like a miniature burst of fireworks. (I had a running dispute with her, as a child, that the sweet-smelling blooms could somehow be converted into either perfume or tea, but all of my chemistry experiments ended up with an odor halfway between cat urine and swamp-gas.)

If you park your car on the gravel curb at this spot, and if you can find a good-sized chunk of rock and heave it directly over the mimosa trees with the strength of a young person, it should disappear and land somewhere near the center of the acreage where my ancestors—Brasfields, and then eventually Allens, Hodges, Shorts, and Tuckers—started putting down roots about 125 years ago.

For posterity, I write down the GPS coordinates: N 33° 40.468, W 87° 05.027.

Who knew?

Other than our family's land, I discovered, the remainder of Shanghi has survived pretty much intact. The centerpiece of the community is still Shanghi Baptist Church, only a half-mile away, whose sprawling, beautifully kept cemetery now extends far past a hillock out back—a space that was formerly woods—toward the old Quinton Post Office. A neighbor of ours, Tommy Howell, once told me it was the only cemetery he'd ever heard of with a waiting list: "I mean, people are just dying to get in there."

I know I should take comfort in the fact that most of the community remains as it was, but oddly enough the opposite is the case. I recall the string of long nights when we sat up watching TV for news of the Cuban Missile Crisis and I actually made my peace with the idea of a world turned to cinders. There was a strangely alluring sense of equality to such a unified demise: no winners or losers, nobody to cluck their tongues and grieve. As it is, my family and its history seem to have been removed from the surroundings here with the precision of a cancer surgeon excising a tumor.

A HISTORY NOTE: I took a photograph of the cooking pot we'd uncovered and posted it on Facebook to ask if anyone had a guess as to the year of its manufacture. There was a quick flurry of replies, people saying their parents or grandparents had the exact cookware: *West Bend / 5-quart / Made in U.S.A.,* and that it was probably sold in the mid-1950s, which fits with my memory.

My grandfather built their house in his "spare time" while they were living in the basement of a concrete-block grocery store (which he had built in his spare time, while working at the coal mine and tending a large garden), along with their daughter, son-in-law, and my colicky asthmatic infant self. I'm guessing that few houses have ever been built with more motivation than theirs was.

I can't remember any member of my family ever having fewer than two jobs at a time. This fact is both inspiring and intimidating to me. Every once in a while I try to imagine the sheer amount of physical labor they expended just to keep my brother and me in food, clothes, and shoes and eventually get us out of the nest. I can't fathom that quantity of work and hopefulness, and at this point I doubt I ever will.

WHEN I TURN THE Honda's ignition key to leave Shanghi, I'm surprised to hear my own voice coming from the radio. It takes my brain a moment to return to current reality, and then I recognize the radio spot promoting a weekly show I do on WJLX-FM in Jasper, featuring Alabama singers and songwriters.

But just as this sinks in, I make a U-turn toward home and the speakers blast only static. In the background a man's voice is shouting, and as I get nearer the Interstate cloverleaf the static subsides enough that the words are audible: "Apostate!...Infidel!...You..." Then the radio tuner resolves itself and I'm hearing, on the same frequency as before, the religious programming my grandparents listened to when I was young. It's a station in Birmingham named WGIB (for "Where God Is Blessing") and I figure the car is roughly equidistant from the two stations' antennas, because the blend of Oldies music, static, and hell-fire sermons shifts back and forth until I'm almost to the city of Cordova, and Oldies wins the battle of the air.

A FEW WEEKS LATER—A Sunday, Father's Day—I'm driving home to Jasper from a business meeting in Birmingham, and on impulse I take Exit 78 toward Shanghi. The sky is cloudless. The parking lot of the church is full, and it's about 10 minutes until the eleven o'clock service starts. It occurs to me that I'm moderately dressed up, which is one rarity, and that I don't have to be someplace in a hurry, another rarity. I go inside and have a seat far in the back just as the pianist starts up on the opening hymn. The gentleman next to me shakes my hand and gives me a songbook. The song is "Power in the Blood," one I know by heart, and from memory I try to sing the bass part like my grandfather did.

The hymn ends, the pastor goes to the podium to make his opening announcements, and when I hear him say my name I'm as startled as I was by the car radio, weeks before. "We'd like to welcome Brother and Sister Brasfield's grandson, Dale," he says, and adds, "Dale, do you have anything you'd like to say?"

For a moment I feel like a first-grader called on by the teacher, but I manage to stand up and say, "No, sir. Just that I'm glad to be here."

"Well," the preacher replies as I sit down, "you've always got a home here."

As he proceeds with the sermon, the lump in my throat grows and grows until the sides of my eyes become wet, and I have to take deep breaths so as not to make a sound.

If it were a perfect world, he would have preached on the Prodigal Son. But I've got nothing to complain about. I know that one by heart, too.

Introduction to the 1988 Edition

To get to Shanghi, Alabama, you take Highway 78 West out of Birmingham. Some twenty miles later you come to the Graysville exit, which you take and then turn left onto Flat Top Road.

In short order you'll pass Flat Top, Bessie Mines, Jonestown, Snowtown, and West Jefferson. A little beyond West Jefferson High School, when you see the reservoir for the power plant on your left, you take a very hard right—almost a U-turn—and find yourself in Twilleytown, a place which was signified at one time by a big railroad trestle which Bobby Adams once hit with his motorcycle. The trestle has since been torn down. Now you can see only the stumps of it and some scattered redrock.

At that point you're almost home. It's a straight shot of about half a mile to Shanghi Baptist Church and Hardin's Grocery, which mark what is roughly the southern boundary of Shanghi. The northern boundary is my grandparents' place—or, if you go the back way called the Old Road, Tommy Howell's house is. Beyond there you've left Shanghi and are in Yerkwood, then Burnwell, and so on until you get to Dora and the main highway again.

I was born and raised in Shanghi. Five generations of my kin have lived there off and on, over the years, in a circle of houses a few hundred yards apart. My grandparents still live there.

How the place got its name is somewhat of a mystery. One version maintains that the community's first church was an architectural innovation, having such a steep, pagoda-like roof that jokesters from neighboring towns started calling it "the Shanghai church," and the name stuck. The church was hit by lightning and burned. Nobody has explained how the second *a* came to be dropped from its Chinese namesake, making it "Shanghi."

It's ironic to me that I spent the first twenty years of my life plotting ways to escape Shanghi for the more glamorous and trend-conscious climes of New York City or Los Angeles, and have spent the second twenty years of my life plotting ways to get back there—if only for a weekend, an afternoon, an hour.

One day last summer I pulled into my grandparents' driveway at about sunset. There was a haze of pollen in the air that made the whole hillside soft and gold-colored, as the sun sank down into the pines and oaks beyond a pole of martin gourds. My grandfather came around the house on his riding lawn mower, taking his time, eating a handful of blueberries he had pulled from the trellis of vines, a ripe plum he had picked from a low-hanging limb.

He saw me and cut the motor. "Sometimes," he said, "this place seems like the Garden of Eden."

I've concurred with that view for years now. The turning point came at age twenty-one, when I found myself farther from Shanghi than I had ever wanted to be—in U.S. Army boot camp at Fort Leonard Wood, Missouri, in the middle of bleakest January with a temperature of three degrees and thirty-five mph winds and, even worse, not a single pine tree in sight.

When I lay down at night in my misery and contrition, the movie of remembrance I saw projected onto the back of my eyelids was not New York or Los Angeles or the paradise of some warm Gulf beach, but Shanghi, Alabama. I would walk all my old woods trails in slow motion and various seasons, one at a time, until blessed sleep came and then the nightmare of morning again, which I survived by counting the hours until I could close my eyes and be back in Shanghi. I promised myself, that terrible and interminable winter, that if I were fortunate enough ever to get back home I would never live more than an hour's drive away from it, if I could help it, until the day I died. So far I've made good on that promise.

It astonishes and saddens me, now, to meet people who have never loved any place in particular, whose home is wherever they're receiving their mail at the moment. To go through life without loving a *place* seems as much a tragedy as not loving a *person.*

When you love someone, you think of them at various times of the day and try to imagine what they're doing at that moment, what they're feeling, what they're looking at. You get pleasure and a strange kind of strength from it.

It's the same with a place. Never a day passes, wherever I happen to be in the world, that I don't picture Shanghi and imagine what the weather is like there, try to gauge from memory the slant of light at that hour on its trees and houses and pastures, the sounds the birds and squirrels and livestock are making, the smells that are in the air.

I've realized, just lately, that whenever I call my grandparents on the phone the first words out of my mouth after "Hello" are "What's the weather doing, there?" I ask it with an urgency that's surprising to me, the way a stockbroker would ask for the latest market report.

What I'm doing, I've realized, is testing against reality the picture of it I've carried in my head all day—erasing lines and colors where necessary, adding others, so that the version I fall asleep with is as accurate as possible.

There's a writer I admire a lot named Wendell Berry. He was raised in a small town in Kentucky which he writes about often. In one book Berry says of a boy growing up there:

> Since the beginning of his consciousness he has felt over and around him the regard of a fellowship of kinsmen and friends, watching him, warning him, fondling him, correcting him, teasing him, instructing him, not so much because of any ambition they have for him as because of where he comes from and because in him they see, come back again, traits and features of dead men they loved.

That durable and loving regard is one of the beauties, maybe the chief beauty, of a place, and it's unfortunate that it's so often invisible to us until after we've gone away.

It's possible to argue, though—an argument I use to comfort myself—that someone who leaves a place and then returns may love it even more (if that's possible) than those who've never left. When the boy in Berry's book grows up and moves away to college and then comes home, he sees the place in a new light:

> And so as he leaves the old house now he steps out into a changed and strangely radiant world, for he is walking now not merely in the place but in his knowledge of it, surrounded by the ghosts and presences of the ones who have cared for him and watched over him there all his life, and he is accompanied by earlier versions of himself that he has lived through. The ache of an exultant sorrow is in his throat.

Having a place like Shanghi to come home to is a far richer birthright than I'm worthy of. Having the privilege of writing about it, and having people in Walker County kind enough to read what I write, is more good fortune than any country boy deserves.

I Left My Heart in Shanghi, Alabama

I

Living in the World

Spring Starts with a Bright Red Motorcycle

Spring arrived this week.

I know the calendar says otherwise. But for me, spring begins on the first sunny day my motorcycle will crank after being cooped up all winter in a tool shed and I'm able to hop on it, my shirttail flapping, and ride down a dirt trail through the woods where a strip pit used to be, scaring brown rabbits and an occasional possum.

I picture myself as a logical and somewhat conservative person. There is nothing logical or conservative about a motorcycle.

Call it a weakness. Especially a trail bike like I have, day-glo red with knobby tires and an engine that has enough cc's to stand you on your head if you're ever foolish enough to give it full throttle in anything less than high gear.

When I was growing up, my mother never would let me have a motorcycle. So, as is true with most vices, when I became self-supporting I got an unbearable urge for one.

I still remember the first *Daily Mountain Eagle* classified ad I answered for a used cycle—some unfortunate person around Morgan's Chapel who told me when I arrived and kicked the tires, "Go ahead. Take a spin on it."

Obviously, he was not aware that I'd never ridden one before. I *had* ridden a *bicycle*, though, and assumed a motorcycle was merely a souped-up version of a bicycle.

Wrong.

A motorcycle weighs about fifty times more, for one thing, a fact that suddenly became important when I stalled the bike at the edge of his driveway and turned it over on my left leg.

I tried my best, but I couldn't lift it. The owner sprinted over and tried his best, too, but being spare of frame as me he couldn't make it budge. I waited, smiling, the circulation in my leg cut off, until he went to get his muscular wife. Among the three of us we finally got the monster upright.

I told them it was certainly a beautiful motorcycle and I'd be getting in touch with them real soon. Whereupon I gave them a false name and headed home as fast as my Volkswagen would carry me.

I've come a long way, both literally and figuratively, since then.

I ended up buying a used Honda that summer, from somebody out past Midfield, and learned to ride it in the privacy of my own driveway. It was copper-colored, metallic flake, and had a four-cylinder motor, 500cc big, that idled so perfectly it sounded like the bass singer in a quartet warming up. Imagine a grasshopper swimming in honey, and you have some idea of how smooth that graceful, angelic motor ran. I've never seen one, before or since, that could match it.

I eventually sold it, of course, like all great remembered things that somehow got away. My son was starting to grow up, and at least half a dozen of my friends hinted to me that selling your motorcycle was a sign of maturity, something I felt in dire need of at the time.

I've repented, over the years, and bought other cycles. But none of them have ever come close to that resplendent, copper-colored Honda.

Until this one.

It's symbolic, I think, that I got a good price on it from somebody whose son was starting to grow up.

Try explaining to a non-rider what a cycle does to your soul, and you find yourself tongue-tied.

Logic doesn't tell you about the dandelion-sized ball of pure joy that explodes in your chest when you point a bike toward the morning sun and ease out the throttle until your bones vibrate with a sound like a gigantic purring cat.

And logic doesn't tell you about all the amazing springtime smells you can ride through in an hour, away from the insulation of a car's air conditioner. Or the way your bare face learns to feel the hundred different temperatures of air as you pass across hills and valleys, like riding up and down through an invisible ocean that nobody but you knows is there.

If you could take pure grace and pure hope and put them on two wheels, you'd lave something that looks a lot like a motorcycle.

It's not logical, I know.

But it's springtime.

What *Are* Movers and Shakers, Anyway?

For a long time I'd been reading articles in newspapers and magazines about "movers and shakers." The movers and shakers in the financial world, in the sports world, in politics, and so on.

Other than the fact that most of the movers and shakers you read about are in their thirties and work for a living, I had no clue to what a mover-and-shaker was. Can you be a mover, but not a shaker, or vice versa? Nobody who writes about these people has ever taken the time to explain it to me.

As with most important concepts, though, I've figured it out myself, the hard way. Just this weekend, as a matter of fact. And I'm glad to enlighten you on the subject, if you're as curious as I was.

It's simple: The "movers" are the people you see every Saturday and Sunday, racing around in borrowed pickup trucks and station wagons, moving their belongings from one house or apartment to another.

Chances are, they're moving because they've (a) taken a new job, (b) gotten fired, (c) gotten married, or (d) gotten divorced.

Or sometimes all of these things at once, which leads you to understand why the movers always look angry or frustrated or frightened—good, ordinary folks pushed to their limits, who are on the verge of committing some violent act you'll read about in the next day's newspaper, which will probably be delivered to their old place and not their new place because they forgot, and so they won't get to read about themselves.

Movers often recruit old friends to help them. Helping somebody move is a more severe test of friendship than it was ever meant to withstand, which makes the mover feel especially guilty before the day is over and much more likely to snap and go off the deep end.

(Is this all starting to make sense, now?)

The "shakers," on the other hand, are people who stand glaring at an office building's thermostat in the summertime, holding themselves by the shoulders and shivering, while cursing the name of whoever set the air conditioning as low as it now is.

Sometimes shakers will take it on themselves to do an informal survey of their co-workers, in an attempt to find out which thoughtless Neanderthal among them is responsible for the resulting cold air. The surveys always come up lacking, in my experience, because no one will confess their air conditioning preferences to a shaker with the wrath of God in his/her eye.

Speaking of gender—movers seem to be equally divided, sex-wise, but int's my observation that most shakers are female. A national study, recently, seems to back this up. On the average, the study found, women prefer a room temperature almost five degrees warmer than men do.

These shakers are the same women, I notice, who are simultaneously wearing (a) very thick, bulky sweaters, and (b) very thin skirts, cut short enough to make frostbite a real threat around any self-respecting air conditioner.

I mean, go figure it.

Anyhow, from now on when you come across an article on the "movers and shakers" in a particular industry, at least you'll know who you're reading about.

No, don't thank me. Really. That's what I'm here for.

Dying of Love: A Common Summer Ailment

Our neighbor's niece is dying this summer.

Dying of love.

It's an ailment you see a lot these summer days, especially among people of the teenage persuasion, as Jenny is.

I suffered from it myself, twenty-odd years ago, but survived. I feel obliged to tell Jenny this—that there's hope for her—but I hesitate because she might misunderstand. Teenagers are very adept at feeling, but not at seeing the bigger picture.

Jenny is from Nebraska or Nevada or somewhere, and has miraculously conned her parents into letting her spend the summer with her thirty-eight-year-old divorcee aunt—most likely on the pretext that the adventure will be educational. Which it is, in ways her parents are most likely having occasional nightmares about.

They would be relieved to know that Jenny is not in love with any*body* in particular. At least not yet.

She's in love with the *idea* of love. The condition is valuable, if excruciating, practice for the real thing.

It causes a young female, for instance, standing in the yard at dusk waiting for the barbecue grill to heat, to dance by herself in a slow, voluptuous dream to music from the radio on the porch, holding herself by the shoulders with great care, unaware that the porch's yellow bug light is spotlighting her for the neighborhood's perusal.

Her aunt, our neighbor, is trying to help. In a way.

She regularly invites teenage boys over to help with the barbecuing. So far they have all been from the same mold: clean-cut, handsome, unthreatening, and with a neck size slightly larger than their IQ.

The girl, for her part, decorates herself with electric-blue eye shadow in a quantity visible from half a block away.

She acts appropriately fascinated with the small talk the muscular boys make; acts enchanted when they use words of more than two syllables, which is rare; acts appropriately helpless with the grill and the charcoal, which she was maneuvering like a pro only days ago when she was dancing late in the yard, alone.

She blinks her artificial eyelashes a lot, making us all fear they will drop onto the hamburgers and be grilled to a crisp.

It's clear she's suffering. Dying, in fact. Of love.

My own near-fatal bout with the affliction took place when I was sixteen.

On the last day of school a girl wrote a full-page message in my yearbook—in pastel green ink, no less—saying that I was a wonderful person and she really enjoyed the time we'd spent together, in class and on field trips, and she only wished it could have been more.

In these days of MTV and explicitness and heavy-metal rock and roll, her inscription would probably be considered pretty tame. At the time, though, when the No. 1 song on the Top 40 was "Happy Together," by The Turtles, such a statement was extremely explosive stuff.

It put me into a daze of love and fear and desperate longing that lasted the whole summer.

I've realized, in the years since, that females have an uncanny knack for giving males great gobs of observation and insight at precisely the time they're most helpless to act on it. Seeing as school was out and I didn't have a car, it would have been very hard to casually drive past her yard and catch her cleaning her barbecue grill, for instance.

The telephone, you say? That occurred to me. I spent most of each long, hot, dry day of that summer mentally composing clever and adorable things to say on the phone. I wasn't quite pleased with any of them, which was just as well because I never got the nerve to call.

No need being hasty, was my motto. But I resolved that on the first day of school I would casually pass her in the hall and invite her to the year's first football game. I carefully sculpted my speech, my offhand air, through a whole stricken, painful summer.

I sat under trees and stared at clouds a lot, with my $5 red plastic transistor radio. Simon and Garfunkel sang, "I am a rock, I am an island . . ." I knew the feeling.

I followed through with my long-considered plan, that long-ago day after Labor Day, with the goldenrod blooming and a slight chill in the air, and the school floors smelling of new cedar wax.

She said no.

She'd been going steady with Mike, she said, for . . . oh, *weeks* now, with a tilt of her small fragile head that said more plainly than any billboard that I'd had my chance and stupidly let it pass.

When I got home that afternoon I pulled the window shades down, put my new Righteous Brothers album on the record player, and skipped supper and cried and felt sorry for myself until bedtime.

We live and learn.

With luck and her aunt's haphazard guidance, Jenny will probably survive the summer.

With even more luck, I can testify, at a time and place when she least needs or expects it, she'll find someone who'll make her whole life snap into place with an almost audible click. And some twenty years down the road, with luck, their daughter will stand in a yard in the twilight, some July evening, tending whatever a barbecue grill looks like by then, and swaying longingly to whatever music the transistor radios will be playing then, and slowly dying. And dying again.

Of love.

Humanity Haunts the Local Laundromat

Think of the sound a cow in a distant pasture makes, calling its calf, in springtime when dusk turns the sky purple and families are coming in home for the night. A soft, questioning sound, sort of "mmmmwuh-h-h?"

That's the sound our washer made last Sunday afternoon, just when we'd put a crucial load of clothes into it, clothes we planned to wear to work and school Monday morning.

No problem, I thought. I'll run to a laundromat.

I remembered laundromats, from my long-ago brief bachelorhood, as bright, cheerful, twenty-four hour places that even a shy person like myself could cope well with, if he remembered the unwritten laundromat rule: Don't stare at the frayed underwear in other people's baskets, and they won't stare at yours.

I drove to the nearest laundromat, unloaded the baskets of clothes from the car, and watched as an elderly man locked the door in front of me. When he saw me, he pointed at my baskets. "No-o-o," he said. "We closin' up."

A laundromat closing in broad daylight? Apparently times have changed.

"Where's the nearest one that's open?" I asked.

"Don't many of 'em open on Sunday," he said. "Except us. And we done closed."

I doubted his word. I drove to two more laundromats. Both closed.

Strange, the way the world works. It used to be hard to find a bank open, but you could go to a laundromat anytime. Now, apparently, the situation is reversed.

As darkness fell, I drove home and consulted the Yellow Pages. One by one, I called a long list of laundromats. No answer. No answer. "We're closing right now." No answer. No answer.

Finally, I reached one who said it would be open for one more hour, but the last load of clothes had to go in within fifteen minutes. I broke the speed limit getting there.

Either laundromats have changed greatly in the past couple of decades, or I have. The place looked dim, lonesome, gloomy.

The people there all looked either young and single or old and alone. Most of the machines sported large "Out of Order" signs. (At least one thing hasn't changed.) The customers stared at a small black-and-white TV with the sound turned down, which sat over the head of a young female attendant, who stared at the clock on the opposite wall and looked as if she'd rather have been anywhere on earth than behind the counter of a laundromat on a Sunday night.

I was surprised, but not really, to see that the machines required three quarters to operate. I remember feeling gypped when they went from one quarter to two.

A big plastic sign said that I could purchase fabric softener from the attendant, but I decided not to press my luck. I'd be lucky to finish by closing time without incurring her wrath. I decided to let my fabrics stay hard.

The girl didn't say a word to anybody, the whole time I was there. But the hand-lettered cardboard signs on the walls spoke volumes about her.

"Please, Please!" one sign was headlined. "Follow These Few Rules!" It enjoined the users of the machines to wipe up their detergent if they spilled it and to use the ashtrays rather than dropping their cigarettes on the floor.

"ALL WE ARE ASKING," the sign concluded, in angry capital letters, "IS SOME BASIC HUMAN COURTESY. WE THINK WE DESERVE IT!!!"

Other signs addressed different points of laundromat etiquette that the customers apparently transgressed often. Like the first sign, the height and angle of the lettering spoke of a silent rage—an occupational hazard, I guess, of watching too many bleary-eyed people in transitional stages of their lives litter your floor with detergent and cigarette butts.

If I had more time, I told myself, and didn't have three loads of wet clothes weighing on my mind, I'd like to hear her side of it, hear what she sees in us, day to day, from her quiet perch beneath the silent TV.

But if I hadn't had crucial wet clothes, I wouldn't have been there in the first place.

We got our washer repaired the next day. The repairman left a note on top of the machine: "SOCK STUCK IN WATER PUMP!" He even attached the offending sock, which looked the worse for wear.

The washer works better than it has in months.

But every time I use it now, I'll think of the quiet, angry girl at the late-night laundromat. And wish her well.

And give thanks that I'm not a regular customer. That I'm no longer single and not yet old and alone.

THESE DOGS PLAY BY THE RULES, AT LEAST

I guess you could say we've worked out a truce.

Not that the dogs lie down and play dead, by a long shot, but at least I'm not as worried, now, about my ankles becoming pork chops as I run through the neighborhood putting in my daily mileage.

It all started before we moved to this house last spring. Before, all my running had been done either on apartment row in Birmingham, where dogs yap at you safely and politely from screen doors and balconies, or out in the woods in Walker County, where a menacing dog can be dealt with properly just before he sinks his teeth into your leg—namely, you can introduce him to a five-pound hunk of redrock without the fear of his owner threatening to sue ("Why, honey, that little ol' rascal won't bite you!")

The first day I donned my shorts and running shoes and took off down the sidewalk here, the dozen or so dogs along our street were the model of courtesy.

No barking. No growling. Apparently because I was new here, they gave me the benefit of the doubt. They sat quietly, heads tilted ever so slightly to one side, like a bunch of accountants giving the first skeptical glance to a new budget proposal.

Great, I thought. Must be so many runners along here, the dogs don't even give them a second thought.

But the *next* day . . .

Yowling and growling and wailing and gnashing of teeth, like the beginnings of a statewide dog war, erupted the instant I got outside our yard. Big dogs, little dogs, gruff dogs, sissy dogs, all in a herd, galloping across lawns and galumphing across vacant lots, all of them seemingly intent on tearing me into strips of sirloin.

But they stopped, inches away, and barked. And barked. And barked.

I picked up my pace considerably, looking around for rocks and sticks and such, but finding none. Maybe they're bluffing, I thought. Maybe their bark is worse than . . .

Sure enough, each of them stood in place a while, yowling and posturing, almost like an actor who has a certain speech to make before going offstage again.

I did what I came there to do: run. And in record time, yet. The dogs did what *they* came out to do, which was to raise a ruckus that could be heard for blocks around.

And we all go through our motions together every day, now, though they've turned their volume down again and I've slowed to a more comfortable trot.

None of them attack, apparently because if they ate a runner they'd have nobody to chase the next day.

Ironically, the loudest and most vicious-looking of the whole pack is the one who stays tied to his owner's porch all the time, with a leash just an inch too short to let him reach the sidewalk. He's a towering, white-haired, huskie-like beast, with a face like a wolf and a full set of teeth he doesn't mind showing.

Any time I see him at his post, I make a detour to the other side of the road. I don't place enough faith in leashes, I guess.

This morning, though, he put one over on me. He was nowhere to be seen when I ventured out, so I trotted through the edge of his yard, which is a mighty convenient shortcut. And then . . . wham, I almost stepped on him, hiding behind a bush.

He never even stood up. I swear he grinned, as if to say, "You owe me one, partner."

Dogs will be dogs, I guess. But it's mighty comforting to know that we live in a neighborhood where the dogs play by the rules.

Doggone comforting.

Eyeing the Inevitable: Rising Rivers, Falling Leaves

The old man was standing in his yard, a cane in his hand and a well-worn baseball cap on his head, looking at his trees and at the sky. The leaves were every warm color imaginable—some the yellow of a thin lemon slice when the sun shines through it, some the snapping orange of a flame, some the mellow reddish-orange of a ripe persimmon. With the wind making them dance against the blue of the sky, they were really something to see.

He had been standing in one place so long that a few of the falling leaves had come to rest against his shoes.

"Ain't it a mess?" he said, when he saw me passing his house. He spanked the carpet of leaves with his cane, making them fly up and then settle down again.

"No use to raking this yard yet," he told me. "They'll just more of 'em fall. May's well wait till they're all gone."

"Aren't they pretty, though?" I said.

He just squinted at the sun. "One time," he said, "there was this river. I was working for the TVA, running a boat, and . . ."

The story was a long, rambling one about the water level being raised, about dams and flooding, about one very old man who had lived in a house near the river all his life and wouldn't sell his property.

"The water will cover your house," lawyers told him. "It'll get you. It's inevitable. You have to give it up."

I listened and followed along, nodding at the right places, and when the story was over he was quiet for a long minute. I told him I thought I smelled dinner cooking, and that I'd better get home.

For the life of me, I couldn't figure out what the rising river in Tennessee had to do with autumn leaves in Alabama.

But I guess when you've lived as many years as he has, you find out that everything that ever happened is connected to every other thing, somehow, and if the person you're talking to can't see the connection there's no use trying to explain it, because he's not old enough yet to see.

He's ninety years old, he says. He still rakes his own leaves and cuts his own grass because he prefers it that way.

His wife has been dead for ten years. He misses her and remembers lots of good things about her, but he never mentions her to me. Only to my wife.

Sometimes his voice cracks and a tear comes in his eye, she tells me, and he has to start talking about something else fast before he cries. Maybe there's an old unwritten rule that men don't talk to men about things that are liable to make them cry.

Seems like I remember reading a story once—or else I dreamed it—about an old Indian chief being stalked for years by death. The chief had been the tribe's finest hunter, in his day, but now he realized that Death was a hunter too, with good eyes and strong legs, while the chief's own eyes and legs were failing. Still, the chief had eluded Death again and again. But with more difficulty each time, with fewer seconds to spare.

What brought it to my mind was watching the old man through the window while we ate.

He stood in the same spot, feet planted firm, watching the setting sun turn itself the same color as the leaves. He held his cane in both hands, the way we hold a stick not to strike out at something but just to defend ourselves from something ahead.

Seems that I remember the Indian in the old story dreading for winter to come, not only because the cold made his bones slow, but because a hunter can see so much farther when the trees are bare.

Or, as I say, maybe I dreamed it all once.

Maybe I'm on the verge of getting old, because I understood, watching the man and the leaves, what an inevitably rising river in Tennessee has to do with inevitably falling leaves in Alabama.

And why our neighbor stands so still, this time of year, looking at the sky.

The Day Mother Found the Cigarettes

Three of us were talking. All of us parents.

We were talking about—as often happens, in that situation—being parents.

It's a rough row to hoe, we agreed.

"I thought when I got to be thirty, I'd have all this wisdom to give my kids," Laura said. "But now I'm thirty, and I just feel like a thirty-year-old kid."

"You never know if you're doing the right thing or not," Chuck put in. "You might not know for years, or maybe ever. What works for one kid won't necessarily work for another."

My addition to the conversation was that the hardest part about being a parent is trying to be consistent with discipline, usually while in the dark about all the facts of a situation. And you secretly hope that other parents won't disagree too harshly with the judgment you impose.

Because kids, after all, are only half the audience you're playing to when you're raising a kid. The other half are other kids' parents.

To help keep us all off guard, there's even a new subject called "parenting," which people are teaching classes and writing books about. I've read a few of the books, but most of their advice covers situations we never encounter in real life with our son.

Maybe if we got him to read the book he'd start choosing more predictable problems.

Two of the strongest weapons on the side of any parent, I'm convinced, are good intentions and dumb luck. It's a career that forces you to fly by the seat of your pants, but most of us manage not to mess up so badly we can't recover from it.

There are some stupid mistakes, some close calls, along the way, though.

And unfortunately our bobbles provide dinner-table conversation for our kids for decades to come. Listen to some barely grown kids, sometimes, comparing Mom-and-Dad stories:

"That's nothing. One time *my* mother . . ."

"You're joking. She didn't do *that* . . ."

"Oh, yes she did."

And so on. The humor, you'll note, is always at the elders' expense.

But few parental legends match the one our neighbor got herself into, a while back. She was passing through her fourteen-year-old daughter's room one afternoon and spotted a pack of cigarettes on the floor beside the bed.

She began preparing her speech immediately, and as soon as she heard her daughter come through the door that afternoon she lowered the boom.

"So you're smoking now?" the momma wailed. "Please, please, *please* don't smoke. Don't wreck your life."

"But, mother . . ."

"I know I haven't been a very good role model, but you don't have to get hooked the way I did. If you never get the habit, you'll never have to fight it. You can quit now, hon. There's still time."

"But I don't . . ."

"You don't have to lie to me. I found these in your room." She held up the evidence.

"Mother?"

"Yes?"

"Those are *your* cigarettes."

"Mine?"

"Remember when we were sitting on the bed talking last night? You must have dropped them.

Silence.

"Oh. Well, never mind."

It's a scene that will be replayed for decades to come, for suitors and school friends and even children and grandkids. The Day Mother Found The Cigarettes.

In fact, the legend has already begun.

I mean, you don't think it was her *mother* who told us about it, do you?

More Rare Than Gold, Silver: A Great Barber

Oil and water. Drinking and driving. Business and pleasure.

To all the things in life which don't mix, as the proverbs tell us, add one more:

Me and haircuts.

I'm not sure if I actually remember my first one, or if the horror stories have been recounted to me so often in family legend that I've imagined a version of it, after the fact.

Anyhow, it must have been a sight to see—me being eased into the barber chair kicking and screaming and, when that didn't get results, bringing in the heavy artillery. Namely, throwing up, with great force and in all directions.

Seems they would have learned, and I would have entered adulthood with waist-length hair, untouched by human clippers since those first unfortunate extravaganzas.

But my parents, and the barber, were stubborn souls.

Make that "barbers," plural. Not many would welcome my production with open arms a second time.

It seems that I would have taken haircuts in stride, with a grandfather and an uncle who'd both been barbers, and the tools of the trade being an everyday part of their households.

But, nope.

Gradually my theatrics lessened. Not that I ever suffered the process gladly.

The short-all-over clip that kids wore in those days was eventually traded for a flat-top, as the 1950s wore on. Maybe that's when I turned the corner from practicality into vanity. Since everybody else had a flat-top (or at least it seemed like it), then it was worth any struggle to maintain one, even though a regular old haircut would have been a lot simpler. (Remember the "training" wax and the plastic brushes, aimed at making your hair stand straight skyward at all times, even if it took on a texture like rubber cement while doing it?)

Enter the Beatles, and flat-tops bit the dust. Long, longer, longest went our hair, and it's plain to see why barbers resented our attitude. While we wanted a quarter-inch or so clipped from the sides, our parents longed for the days of flat-tops and neatness and Lawrence Welk. And since they were paying for the haircuts, we pouted and submitted and made it plain we were doing it under protest. The poor barber was the reluctant middleman to the transaction.

One barber I knew, back then, had a sign in his window that said, "TAKE A LOAD OFF YOUR MIND: GET A HAIRCUT."

A strange thing happened when I started paying for my own haircuts.

I began going to great lengths (if you'll pardon the expression) to tell the barber exactly how I wanted the finished product to look. Even bringing pictures, if necessary. I mean, when it comes to being acceptable looks-wise, some of us need all the help we can get. So I desperately enlisted my barber's aid in that effort, hoping some unwary female might be inclined to overlook the part of me below the hairline if the top inch was attractive enough.

But the barbers repeatedly cut off too much (prompting me to consider wearing a sign, afterward, saying "Yes, I DO have a new haircut, and yes, he DID cut off a lot; I realize this, but all I can do is wait for it to grow back"). Or else they didn't cut off enough. Or else too much in the wrong places.

I told a barber once, "Gee, I hate to complain, but that's not anything like the way I said I wanted it."

The barber shrugged. "Yeah, I know," he said. "But I think this way looks better."

Well, thank you, sir. That's good to know. I guess.

Ah, me.

My search for the perfect barber extended to out-of-the-way places, to shopping centers, to downtown offices decorated like Old English palaces or Old West saloons. No luck.

I even tried the shops with ten or twelve barbers in a row—cartoon characters all over the walls, coffee perking, bubblegum everywhere in bowls, and heavy-metal music so loud I could still feel the boomp-boomp-boomp of the drum long after leaving.

And then I tried Butch Courington.

And my search was over.

"You drive to *where* to get your hair cut?" people ask. "That's a long way."

Yep, but I've *come* a long way, and by the time you get a white hair for every black one, you can appreciate somebody who knows what he's doing, with no frills or circus decorations or boomp-boomp-boomp.

That's Butch.

And if I pick up a little advice there on real estate or taxes or a good place to take a vacation, so much the better. This week he even told me the unsettling news about a customer not much older than either of us who's in the hospital for emergency bypass heart surgery, which he didn't even know he needed until he went for a checkup.

Which left me to ponder what I'd do if Butch ever quit barbering or moved to Alaska or got hit by a truck or something.

And which reminded me that, good as I feel, I'm a bit overdue for a checkup myself.

Butch is planning to get one, too.

And that's a load off my mind.

Crowd Turns aside from a Mother's Prophecy

Noontime, and the city streets were an anthill of people, driving and walking and running, trying to get to the bank before lunch, and then back to work on time, and then home, and then . . . busy, busy.

Over all the noise, one loud voice could be heard. If you looked around, the speaker wasn't hard to spot amid the crowds in bright polyester and knotted neckties.

An elderly black woman . . . eighty, ninety? . . . so thin she looked like a broom that had come to life. Her head-rag and long dress and apron all looked to have been made from printed cloth at one time, but they had long faded to a grayish-brown, like tree bark, so that the flower pattern hardly showed at all.

She carried a walking cane of rough-whittled wood—more like a staff, really, the long kind of stick you see in Bible pictures—and she was shouting. Preaching. Shaming anyone who would look her in the eye.

No one would.

"She took care of you, didn't she?" the old woman shouted. "Took GOOD care of you, your momma did. Fed you and wiped you when you couldn't even stand on you feet. Ain't that right, now? Tell me!"

The hurrying walkers, people coming and going from the offices and stores and warehouses along the street, seemed to ignore her as they passed, but when they got at a safe distance they stopped and turned to stare. And then glanced at each other, some of them giggling nervously.

"And what did you do for HER, this woman who give you your life and give you her life too? You run off and leave her. You LEAVE her. That's what, people. Ain't I true, now? Look at me!"

The straightness of her figure was bowed forward, very slightly, as if she were being blown by the memory of some old, strong wind as she walked.

People leaving buildings, people who had to cross her path to get to their parked cars, got in those cars quickly and rolled the windows up, despite the heat, and drove off faster than was safe, all trying to avoid her as if she were someone dangerous.

"You . . . live . . . too . . . FAST, people!" she shouted, and slammed her walking stick against the concrete so hard it must have shot pain through her bony arm. "You don't see what you doin'! Lord God, you MUST not be seein' what you doin', people!"

She kept to her path, up the center of the crowded sidewalk, while vacant-eyed shoppers and workers parted in front of her walking stick like some Red Sea of humans and then joined again when they'd gotten past her.

"You momma was GOOD to you, weren't she, now? She SACRIFICED for you! Huh, now, boy? Tell me if I'm lyin'! Huh, boy?"

The "boy" she is speaking to is a businessman who looks to be about sixty years old. He is suddenly taken by a coughing fit, it seems, so that his eyes are closed when he goes past the woman. He quickens his step.

"She loves you like a BABY, and then what do you do but leave, huh? What but leave? Godamighty . . ."

Every few steps she spins around on one foot, almost falling and then propping anew with her stick, so that her voice carries in all directions.

"You live too FAST, people! You must not SEE! God's WRATH gonna come! Hear me, now! Hear me!"

If anyone hears, they show no sign of it.

They pass her, faster than before.

And she keeps on, like a broom walking.

Victims of Pure Racket, Take Heed: Try Earplugs

About four o'clock every morning, the symphony starts on the hillside where we live.

Not Bach or Beethoven. Just pure racket.

First, usually, there's a fire truck or two. And just as the fire gets put out and you almost get back to sleep, an ambulance careens through.

Apparently the ambulance serves as a signal to all the cats in the neighborhood that it's time to gather for their nightly free-for-all.

Once the feline vocal extravaganza begins to die down, along about 5:00 a.m., the garbage trucks start rolling—the kind with the big motorized arms that snatch a giant metal trash dumpster straight up and wham it against the top of the truck several times to make sure it's all emptied.

I'm not saying the process is loud, but I have it on good authority that several of the folks over in the cemetery think seriously, about that time, of getting up and having breakfast.

When all the garbage trucks clear out, at about five-thirty, the birds go into action, singing their little feathered hearts out—which would ordinarily be a truly enriching experience to hear, except when you've been lying awake since four o'clock knowing you have to get up at six.

Fortunately, the wonders of modern technology have provided an answer to such a dilemma as mine:

Earplugs.

I invested in a pair of them a couple of weeks ago. There's a lot to be said for earplugs, both pro and con.

That's why I've put together this brief user's guide, in case you're considering taking the big step yourself:

(1) SHOP AROUND.

The first three places I shopped had the paraffin-type earplugs that look like wads of Juicy Fruit gum. All you have to do, the druggist said, is mold them into little plugs, get them warm with your fingers, and stick them in.

That idea bothered me. My theory is that if you have something that soft and waxy and pliable up inside your ear, there's nothing to stop your body heat from liquefying it some night and letting it seep into your brain, where it might harden again and permanently plug up the circuits you use for such critical activities as tasting collards and listening to George Jones albums. I couldn't hack that.

Finally I tried a distributor of industrial safety supplies, whose earplugs were green and orange rubber and looked like a cross between a spark plug and E.T.'s fingers. They're made to block out such loud noises as giant factory drill presses, diesel motors, and so on. Heavy-duty stuff.

"But what about mockingbirds and cat fights?" I asked the sale clerk.

"Say what?" she said.

I bought a pair.

(2) PRACTICE MAKES PERFECT

The first time you attach a set of serious earplugs, you feel like you have a spark plug in one ear and E.T.'s finger in the other. "I can't sleep like this," you'll say to yourself.

Leave them in a while, though, and you'll forget about them entirely, believe it or not. A few nights later, just as you're saying to yourself, "I can't sleep like . . ." that will be all she wrote.

(3) APPOINT A SHAKER

Earplugs prevent you from hearing the alarm clock too, unfortunately, so it's necessary to appoint somebody in your household to listen to your alarm clock for you and come shake you violently when it goes off. Most likely this will scare you so badly you'll jump straight up and your eyes will boog 'way out, an entertainment which will more than repay them for their trouble.

(4) REPEAT OVER AND OVER, "I AM NOT DEAF."

The first few mornings you see your wife's mouth moving and no sound coming out, you'll panic and think you've gone deaf in the night. You'll get over it.

(5) BE AGREEABLE

If you ordinarily spend your first waking hours in such concentration-requiring tasks as studying, writing, or doing bookkeeping, you'll probably find it useful to keep your earplugs in for that. Inform the people in your house of this but don't expect them to remember. They will talk to you right on.

Don't succumb to the temptation to take your earplugs out and ask them to repeat what they said. They will get angry, because they forgot. Instead, if you see your wife's mouth moving, wait until it stops and then furrow your forehead and say, "You're probably right." You may even find that earplugs improve your marriage.

These hints should get you started.

If there are no further questions, then, we'll . . .

Say, WHAT?

ONE GOOD REASON TO FEEL SORRY FOR WOMEN

It's a grim sight.

Every morning, on the way to my office, I meet an endless stream of cars coming over the mountain toward downtown. All the men at the wheel look like . . . well, like men on their way to work. But the *women* . . . oh, it's sad to see. They're gorgeous.

Bound for work, they look to be just fresh from their makeup mirrors—radiantly toned faces, every hair in place, clothes the color of muted autumn leaves, their ruffled collars standing up clean and crisp as white flowers.

But the expression on their faces, almost without exception, is grimness and misery and dread, like exhausted soldiers going once again into battle.

Having never been either beautiful or a woman, myself, I'm forced to guess at the reason.

It would be easy to say they dread going to work, and leave it at that. They don't dread it any more than I do, I maintain, so I suspect the real reason is more complicated. Otherwise, dressed-up women would look happy and relieved on their way home at evening (which they don't), or walking into a restaurant at night, or headed for church on Sunday morning.

I suspect that when you grow up, as American women do, surrounded day and night by billboards and magazine covers and TV commercials featuring larger-than-life faces of models radiantly fresh from their makeup mirrors, every hair in place, it's only natural to assume that the American way of life is to look that way whenever anybody's watching. Or might be watching, which is most all the time.

Being crisp and radiant, I'd imagine, is a full-time job.

Compare the length of the lines outside the men's room and ladies' room, and you get some idea of the magnitude.

If I were a woman I'd probably resent the whole state of affairs, though I probably wouldn't admit it. If I were a woman, I imagine I'd try to perpetuate the myth that being "fixed up" came as naturally as breathing to someone of my gender, and that it was no trouble at all to peer into every reflective surface, day and night, to check myself over and maintain that state of visual grace.

A great-great-uncle of mine, I'm told, who's long dead now, took great pleasure in startling a crowd by announcing loudly, "I feel sorry for women!"

And when he had everybody's attention, he would conclude, "They go to so much trouble to be beautiful. Why, all I have to do in the morning is put on a clean pair of overalls, and I'm beautiful!" He'd wink, then, and slap his hands together and laugh out loud at himself.

The women's reaction to all this is, unfortunately, lost to history.

In past months, I have seen women attempt to maintain a radiant and crisp demeanor while (A) running ten miles on a ninety-degree day, (B) cooking a large meal in an oven and on a stovetop, (C) playing five fierce games of racquetball in a row, and (D) lifting weights for an hour.

These are all wonderful and laudable things for human beings to do—especially females, with their traditional societal constraints of appearing fragile, elegant, and lace-draped (except for the hours of the day, of course, when they were cooking, cleaning, washing, and hoeing).

And I admit there is some bizarre attraction in watching a frail woman run past me like I was standing still—a woman with eye liner and mascara, blush, lipstick, tiny gold stars in her ears, a gold necklace as delicate as a spider web, and who leaves in her wake the scent of fresh spring flowers.

Unlike me.

Still, it frightens me to contemplate what women would be capable of if they didn't have to spend so much of their time and energy staying beautiful, even while sweating like a plow-horse.

I don't mean to look a gift horse in the mouth. Being gorgeous is . . . well, gorgeous. In its place.

But apparently nobody's told women that they're most beautiful at those rare times in their life when they don't know anybody's looking. When they've not arrayed themselves for battle, when their hair is out of place and their cheeks are red from exertion and maybe a drop of sweat is hanging from the tip of their nose and they're looking into the distance thinking intently about what they're doing at that instant.

Thinking about anything, that is, except being beautiful for whoever's watching.

Now, *that's* a sight to see.

Brooke Is More Fun Than TV

The hour was late, and my brain was even more weary than usual. As I sat hunched over the typewriter the client's voice came back to haunt me, from a meeting earlier that day about the script he wanted:

"We need something really dramatic for the beginning, I'm not sure what. Just use your imagination. Needs to be really straightforward, really brief, but . . . catchy, you know? Something memorable. And save something really snappy for the ending. Big finish, you know? Something jazzy, with impact, for them to remember as they leave, OK? You can whip us up something by tomorrow, can't you? Huh? Sure you can. See you then, all right?"

Now, though, as the sun went down, the only marks on my typing paper were two giant drops of sweat. No blood, yet, although tears weren't an impossibility. I began to suspect that my imagination, after cranking out pretty good stuff night and day for the past couple of weeks, had sneaked off to the beach without me.

As a last resort, I fled into the living room and turned on the TV to a channel at random, hoping that a few minutes of drab summer rerun would suddenly make writing seem a tempting alternative. In other words, I was killing time.

That's when Brooke came over.

Brooke lives next door. She's nine and has blond hair and freckles and a tiny, elegant socialite nose that looks exactly like the sketched profiles in the magazine ads that ask, "Can You Draw This Face?" Brooke looks as though a country club membership is laid up for her somewhere, on the basis of looks alone, awaiting her adulthood.

The TV movie consisted of several obnoxious teenagers saying a wide range of dumb and stereotyped things while trying to look extremely cool and detached. And, anyway, Brooke said she'd already seen it.

"When I get married," Brooke said, with no introductory statement, "I'm going to live in a mansion."

Keeping one eye on the obnoxious teens, I nodded and said a mansion would be nice.

"I'm going to be a nurse when I grow up," she said. "I think I'll be good at it. I took a splinter out of Margaret's foot one time, with a needle, and she said it hardly even hurt, so now other kids come to me when they need something taken out, and I've kind of gotten to be the neighborhood nurse."

I told her that nursing would be a wonderfully satisfying career but that nurses in general didn't make enough money to live in mansions.

"Well, that's OK," she said, "because I'm going to be a dance teacher and a singer and an actress, too."

"Oh," I said.

"And a professional swimmer."

"Mmm," I said.

"And my husband's going to look sort of like *that,*" she said, pointing to the face of the least obnoxious teenager in the movie. "He's going to be a lawyer and a doctor and an architect."

I suggested they'd be a pretty busy couple.

"We can give tours of the house, too, like Disneyland, because it's going to have a roller coaster through the bedroom, and a big slide at the back porch, so that when you open the back door you sli-i-i-ide down onto a trampoline, and the trampoline bounces you into the swimming pool."

I mentioned that her mansion didn't sound like a very good place for just resting or reading a book.

She shrugged, as if to say that some things can't be helped. Considering that she has a brand-new baby brother at home these days, still in diapers, I decided that a roller coaster through the bedroom might seem restful by comparison.

"And the front door will play 'Yay, Alabama!' when you ring it," she said. "Or you can tell it to play any song you want to, depending on who's coming. But nobody for Auburn's going to be invited to my house, just people for Alabama. And upstairs I'm going to have cats and dogs and elephants and monkeys and lions."

I suggested that she ought to start looking for a high grade of carpet.

"Oh, we'll have a maid to clean up after the animals," she said. "She'll have a little shovel with diamonds on it. We'll call her 'Scoop.'"

"Mmm," I said.

"And we'll have diamonds in the bathroom, too, on the walls and the sink and everywhere, except that the ones on the seat will have to be sanded down or something, you know? And the bathroom tissue will always be the holiday kind, like for Christmas and New Year's and Fourth of July and Halloween and Thanksgiving . . ."

"And Groundhog Day?" I mused.

". . . and Groundhog Day, with pictures of little groundhogs popping up out of their holes like this . . ." She stuck her finger in her mouth and made a loud, percussive POP, which she followed with a credible imitation of a groundhog.

"And all my children can take dance classes at Corky Bell's, and they can invent a dance called The Moolah, and I'll have a hairdresser who raises me up on pillows in the morning, and fixes my hair without hurting, except I won't have anybody who bathes me, because that's tacky, and besides, nobody but yourself can get in all the creases good, I think."

I couldn't argue with that. Suddenly I imagined I heard my prodigal imagination knocking weakly at the back door, home from the beach a week early.

That was when Brooke allowed that her mother was probably wondering where she was, so she'd better head back.

"Brooke," I said, as she scampered out the door, "you're more fun than TV."

"I know," she said.

2

Heart and Home

When the Time Is Right: A Grafting of Lives

Maybe it's the grove of white-blossoming cherry trees along this hillside, on the verge of spring, that brings the comparison to mind.

But I've been thinking all week about seeing a row of grafted trees, when I was very young. One kind of limb had been cut into place on another kind of trunk, and there was a knot of something hard and waxy-looking (paraffin, maybe) covering the joined place, protecting it until the new bark could grow.

I remember that the sight sent chills up my back, the way seeing an open cut in someone's skin does. I suppose I figured the trees must have been in pain, even though knowledge and logic told me otherwise.

It's very late at night, now, and there is no sound in this house but me. I've just walked through all the darkened rooms again, a low moon the only light, and looked at all the boxes in the floor, on tables, on shelves. And it slowly dawns on me, all over again, what Saturday holds: flowers, candles, organ music, a church full of friends, a woman in a white lace gown. All planned, in the depths of winter, for the first full day of spring.

The moonlit boxes contain our separate histories, hers and mine. The long and complex string of events has led us to one place, where we agree on one large thing. That fact is as amazing to me as college algebra classes used to be, when a professor named Bishop who looked for all the world like W. C. Fields would stand at the blackboard and do "identities." A big complicated formula would be scrawled on the left, then an equals sign, and we'd hold our breath for the mess of numbers and symbols that was sure to follow on the righthand side.

But he'd fool us.

"Equals . . . one," he'd write, and grin because he had known the secret all along. I never understood, and still don't, how so many complicated things can balance into one so simple.

The books and records and clothes and dishes and window shades and flower pots and picture frames of two households have not been here even one month, and already it's hard to remember which place each one came from.

At this late hour, I finally understand the uneasiness that has been with me tonight. Namely, that the grafting of all these things, and our two lives, has not been painful to us at all. No doubts. No jitters.

Even though that's the question everyone's asking us this week, only half in jest: "No second thoughts, huh? Not ready to back out?"

It seems odd, I know, and disturbing, in a world where pairs of lives splinter every day by the thousands, like rotted wood. The unshakeable certainty that ours won't is either foolishly wrong or very, very right. There aren't any guarantees.

A Kentucky English teacher named Wendell Berry has written lots of books about the good old days, and the healing power of sun and rain and seeds and an acre of land. He says in one of his books that our lives have gotten fragmented in the past half-century because we've broken away from the natural cycle of things, away from the land and the seasons, and we now hesitate to do things like plowing and planting seeds because nobody can guarantee us that we will prosper.

"Long ago," Berry says, "a farmer did not plant seeds because they would grow into crops or the crops would sell for money. A farmer planted seeds because it was the time of the year to do so, and because it would be unthinkable not to."

Looking from here, from now, Saturday's ritual seems as inevitable and as necessary as a sunrise or a good rain. Then, following it, comes a week far from both our pasts, with only seagulls and salt water for company. It will serve the same purpose, I guess, as the circles of paraffin on those long-ago freshly joined trees.

As for what follows that, nobody knows. Least of all us.

As for now, though, it's time.

Aging Cat Helps Fend Off Squirrel Invasion

We've been invaded.

Word must have gone out this fall, among squirrels, that the Shorts' backyard is a particularly good place to be.

Squirrels scamper up and down our tree trunks, hold cross-country races on the roof, climb to the top of saplings no bigger around than your thumb and cling there, delighted, while the little trees whipsaw back and forth almost to the ground, like a new amusement park ride.

They do high-wire acrobatics on our TV cable. They walk right up the cable, to where it joins the house, and they stare in the window at us, eye to eye, while we're eating breakfast. Sometimes they look a little wistful about the prospect of scrambled eggs and toast, seeing as their jaws are pooched out with a big shiny acorn which is bound for their deep-freeze, not for eating.

Maybe it's my imagination, but it seems that squirrels are bigger and healthier than they used to be. I'd always thought of them as scrawny, refugee-looking animals, but the ones in our yard this year are as big and sleek as house pets.

The squirrel invasion is OK with me.

The only member of our family who seems in the least distressed with it is our somewhat aging cat, Buttermilk.

Buttermilk knows instinctively that no matter how cute and frisky squirrels are, the dictionary will tell you that they're "rodents"—first cousins of the ugly, slick-tailed gophers that climb around on trash piles at night. And she treats them accordingly. With great disgust, that is, except when she has a chance of catching and eating one.

Since Buttermilk's fur is roughly the same color as a pile of dry leaves, she does a lot of lurking in the edges of the yard these days, hoping a squirrel will overlook her and come down to earth—or at least to a low-hanging limb—long enough for her to get her claws into him.

At one time I would have discouraged her from doing that—a long time ago, when I was twenty-one years old and had appointed myself protector of the moral order of the universe, helping poor wayward animals and plants see the error of their instinctive ways.

In general, back then, whenever I tried to butt in on nature, nature came out the loser. I eventually grasped the meaning of a phrase I'd heard all my life—"Let nature take its course"—and things went a lot smoother after that.

Nowadays if cats want to eat squirrels, or vice versa, I figure it's pretty much their own business.

Fortunately for the local squirrels, though, Buttermilk isn't as young as she used to be. She moves a lot slower and doesn't jump nearly as high. The expression on her face tries to pass it off as a newfound gracefulness she's acquired with her maturity, but it's probably just arthritis.

For all her investment of time in careful lurking, only one squirrel has bitten the dust this year, as far as we know.

One evening when we got home from work and went out to feed her, she had laid a carefully gnawed squirrel skeleton beside her food bowl for us to see. Considering how plump and healthy these squirrels are, she must have had quite a wrestling match before she overpowered it.

She didn't touch her dry cat food that night. She yawned and smiled and lot and took some long naps. Her mouth looked greasy.

The next day, my wife mentioned Buttermilk's kill to a friend of ours. "Isn't that something?" my wife said, "For Buttermilk to catch a squirrel, and her so old?"

Suzanne seemed unimpressed.

"How old was the squirrel?" she asked.

Buttermilk won't say.

The Signs of Summer's End Are Upon Us

This month, all the signs of summer's end seem to pop up at once, everywhere. But more likely it's just because I've started watching for them.

If only we weren't forced by the stresses of earning a living to put on blinders, most days, to everything nature does.

If only we could be advanced enough to appoint someone as a "shaman" the way primitive cultures do—a person to watch the everyday things around us for signs of what's to come. A shaman around our household would probably have spotted, in slow stages, over the past couple of weeks, what I didn't see until today:

– Our backyard is inhabited by locusts. Or inhabited by locust *shells,* rather: the crisp, dry ghost of them. They're the color and consistency of the fried pork skins we used to buy off a counter rack at the grocery store and wash down with a Grapico.

The locusts themselves are long gone, of course, having escaped their old bodies through a razor-like slit in the back.

(They told us in high school literature that some creatures actually do change bodily lodgings as they outgrow themselves—remember the poem about the chambered nautilus?—but I don't think the full impact on that has dawned on me yet. Maybe it won't until I wake up one morning and see that my own hands and face have gone dry and transparent with age.)

Unnamable critters, bizarrely shaped insects I've never seen before, are slowly stalking about our house and yard as though they're lost or have suffered such a sadness that their minds are not on what they're doing.

As I raised up from reading a book this morning, I came nose to nose with an olive-colored monster half as big as a fist, all legs and horns and angles. By reflex I smashed him with the book, and I didn't realize until later that he hadn't even tried to run.

—The real souvenirs of summer aren't the ones you buy at gift shops—the pennants and coffee cups and tiny hardwood plaques with the names of cities embossed on them.

The real souvenirs are the ones you come upon in unexpected places as the world makes its frantic downhill slide into September. The dried banana peel hiding in the bottom of a picnic basket, souvenir of a Saturday trip to the lake. Scraps of paper scribbled with reminders of the hundred tasks that had to be done before taking off on vacation. A novel with its page turned down at the place just before the real killer confesses, making you realize the killer has been crouching inside the cramped book since May, just itching to tell all, and in the meantime you've forgotten who he killed.

Summer's like that.

—The last remaining evidence of my best-ever summer employee is slowly dwindling. Every morning I find on my office desk a few more fallen petals from the rose in the Burger King cup, as the employee himself endures the rigors of fourth grade, barely a mile from here.

I remember the noontime a week ago when he came down the sidewalk with a sack of lunchtime hamburgers in hand. His other hand was behind him, befitting a surprise.

When he came through the door he held out the rose, and suddenly the pressures and frustrations of my day vanished into the rose-smelling air.

"I stopped at the florist to see how much the roses were," he explained, "and the lady said they were three dollars. I told her thanks anyway, but I just had two dollars left. So she said, in that case, she could give me a smaller rose for two dollars."

I told him I was glad it happened that way.

He looked at me with the patience of a long-suffering adult. "No. See? It wasn't *really* a smaller rose," he confided. "She just said that because I was a kid and she wanted to be nice to me."

"Ah," I allowed.

We took time for a longer-than-usual hug. And then I went to hunt a container for a thirsty rose, hoping that with a little luck it would outlast summer. But nothing does.

Except the memories.

Nothing Lifts Your Spirits Like a Slingshot

I had gone into the sporting goods store to pick up some jogging socks. But in order to get to the checkout counter, I had to pass a display rack filled with "impulse" items.

If you've ever been in the retail business, you know that an impulse item is anything a customer didn't come looking for, but which you try to sell him (or her) anyhow.

Goodness knows I didn't come shopping for a slingshot. But I came away with one, just the same.

"Ah-hah," the clerk commented. "Going to do some bird hunting, huh?"

"Oh, no," I answered him. "I just . . ."

That's when it occurred to me that I had no idea what I was going to DO with the thing. I just knew that some spot way down inside me had itched, very badly, when I passed the rack of slingshots.

As I left the store, I started to put the slingshot in my back pocket. But I had sudden visions of Dennis the Menace with his ever-present trademark, so I put mine in a plain brown sack instead.

Driving home, it dawned on me that there is no reasonable excuse for a grown man to spend an hour in the woods shooting at trees with a slingshot—something which I suddenly wanted, very badly, to do.

No excuse, that is, but one.

One of the fringe benefits of having a seven-year-old son is that you, too, can act seven years old from time to time, without having people look at you funny.

Donovan's reaction, out loud, was just what my reaction had been, inwardly, when I first saw the thing.

"A slingshot!" he said. "Who-o-o-E-E-E!!!"

And so we were off.

The woods were dappled with sun; a fine breeze was blowing. Birds were singing when we got there. When they saw us they quickly sized up our marksmanship abilities and kept their perches, singing right on.

Donovan and I weren't choosy about ammunition. We shot little rocks, big rocks, middle-sized rocks, round rocks, square rocks, flint rocks, shale rocks, and even a few rocks that were probably, had their pedigree been known, actually dirt clods in disguise.

We shot at tree trunks, at leaves, at the ground, at the sky, and even at a couple of tin cans we propped on a rock ledge.

If we had stayed until dark we'd probably have taken a shot or two at the moon.

At twilight, as we sat in an ice cream shop sharing a healthy platter of Rocky Road, peach, and chocolate, I had a chance to wonder at just what it is about being male that holds such a fascination for slingshots.

At the risk of offending the new wave of thinkers who maintain that maleness and femaleness are really one and the same deep down, I think that the answer is this:

There's something in a boy or a man that aches to mark things, to hit at things. Far-off things.

Not in a destructive way, necessarily. Just a striving—a nameless, aching striving. An over-whelming desire to master heights and depths and distances. Even if "mastering" means, for the moment, only pinging them with a small flint rock. It's in our blood, somehow.

"One more time?" Donovan asked, warily, eyeing the slingshot I had by now transferred to my back pocket, the image of Dennis the Menace notwithstanding.

Sure, partner. One more time.

Then, maybe, the moon.

The Twenty-Year Reunion (We Looked Almost Normal)

WEST JEFFERSON—There was a copy of the school newspaper taped on the door of the lunchroom. *The Crimson Tattler,* dated 1967. The hallway of West Jefferson High School smelled exactly as it had smelled twenty years ago this month, when we were rehearsing for graduation. The lingering odor of chalk dust and books and countless lunches and exhilaration and lust and heartbreak. Your standard high school smells.

Standing there with my hand on the doorknob, at two o'clock in the afternoon, I had the sudden uneasy feeling that I was trapped in a time warp. (It was like the recurring dream I have, that through some bureaucratic oversight I am back in boot camp again and nobody will listen to my story that I'm thirty-seven years old and have a wife and son and official discharge papers at home, if they'll only let me go get them. "Get back in line, Short," the drill sergeant says, in the dream, and I sigh and march away.)

Then I turned the doorknob and stepped into the lunchroom and saw, to my great relief, that it was still 1987 after all. Jane and Jannice and Nolan and Roy and Sarah and the others all looked twenty years older, just like I did. Seeing them was like the feeling you get when you see the lights of your grandparents' house after driving a long way in a storm. Everything is all right now, you tell yourself. I'm home.

A friend of mine who went to her twenty-year reunion last year told me that it renewed her faith in nature. There really is justice, she said. After twenty years, most of the beautiful people in her class had begun to get bald spots and wrinkles and put on a few extra pounds. The formerly pudgy or plain or bashful, meanwhile, had trimmed down and glamored up and looked healthy and successful.

It's not a hard and fast rule, I discovered, but it's true often enough to warm one's heart.

We drank strong coffee and ate snacks and introduced our wives and husbands to each other while the video camera rolled. But mostly we watched each other in open amazement.

Roy is a structural engineer, now. Chester works for the phone company. Roger does geological consulting. One Glynda is in the video business, the other Glenda is a church secretary. George is in the army. Bobby is a preacher. Jane is a medical technician. Alana is in real estate.

And so on.

A good number of us are divorced at least once. Miraculously, none of us are dead or in prison, fates that we were threatened with countless times by our parents and teachers.

Speaking of teachers, Mrs. Howard showed up. And Mrs. Lollar.

I couldn't resist telling Mrs. Howard how much I'd come to appreciate her classes in civics and history, in the years since. She taught us how the government worked and how we should support it when it acted right and raise an almighty fuss when it acted wrong. Back then, whenever some president or general or senator would try to pull a fast one, Mrs. Howard would harken us back to the Constitution, and show us in stern black-and-white where the culprit had gone wrong and how such infractions could be prevented in the future if we stayed on our toes. Till this day, whenever I read a newspaper, a part of me is wondering what Mrs. Howard would say about the latest developments.

I couldn't resist telling Mrs. Lollar I was glad she'd made us act somewhat civilized in her library, those years, insisting that we return books on time and refrain from shouting dumb things while people were trying to read.

If Miss Smith had been able to come, I'd have thanked her for unselfishly teaching me great quantities of algebra and calculus far beyond the call of duty, back when I (mistakenly) planned to be an aeronautical engineer. I'd have thanked Mr. Weems for passing on to us his fascination with science. And I'd have thanked Mrs. Huffman for teaching us to diagram sentences and for instilling in me the odd idea that I could make a living writing the English language—a concept more strange to me, back then, than flying to the moon.

But before long it would begin getting dark outside, and on the pretense of looking for a restroom I snooped through the old building at sunset, peering in classroom doors and trying to conjure up, in the silence, how it had been.

I don't know what I was expecting. The rooms were just rooms. The desks were just desks. The shelves were just shelves—unlike back then, when every pencil and windowpane and stick of wood had seemed charged with high drama, with unlimited possibility, with breathtaking emotional significance.

Maybe it was just a hormonal problem.

Or maybe we took the drama, the possibility, the emotions, all with us, like picking a roasted turkey clean, forcing the next class to start from scratch and create their own.

"I just can't get over it," Sarah said to me, when I went back to the gathering. "Everybody looks so . . ." She stopped, looking out over all of us, not sure of the word she wanted. But I could tell what she thinking.

"So . . . *normal*," she finally said, and laughed. And I had to admit she was right.

Miracles happen.

There's No Place Like a New (Old) Home

It's a little scary, waking up here.

The alarm rings and I reach to shut if off, but my hand hits only air. I sit up in bed and realize that somebody has moved everything around while I slept. The bedside tables are different. There's a window where the wall was, and vice versa. Welcome to the Twilight Zone.

Then it gradually dawns on me that we have a new house. And that everything's all right.

Better than all right, actually.

We had the good fortune, a couple of months ago, to find the house we'd looked for, in vain, for about seven years. And the even better fortune that the person living in it had to move, and quick.

Here she was, just freshly married to somebody from up North, and was willing to let a wonderful house go, at a good price, just to be with her sweetie. I guess there's no accounting for taste.

I still remember the sweltering Sunday afternoon when Mary came home from the grocery store and said, "I found us a house."

To say I was skeptical is an understatement. We had plodded through enough houses in the past several years to thoroughly sicken us out on the species.

It's not like we were asking for something unreasonable—just a regular old two-story house, nothing fancy, built maybe in the 1920s or so, with floors sturdy enough not to cave in, a layout with enough space that we could stretch our three selves out at random without bumping into things, and with a price tag considerably less than Sheik What's-His-Name paid for his latest yacht.

Such an animal was not to be found.

Until now.

We drove over to look at it that afternoon, just about sunset. We stood on the hillside above it and, after an exhaustive inspection of ten seconds or so, I felt the strange tickling just behind my breastbone that has always accompanied the treacherous process of falling in love.

Our real estate agent, bless her, led us through at a slow pace the next day, basement to attic, pointing out what she considered the most important features: the new heatpump, the dishwasher, the carpet, the termite inspection bond, and so on and so forth.

Even though the *really* important features, as she probably knew, are the ones you can only discover for yourself after you've moved in and it's too late to reconsider.

A little like marriage, in a way.

The initial honeymoon with the house must be over, because every day this week I've discovered something about it I didn't know when I moved in. Some are good, some bad. (A *lot* like marriage, actually.)

On the minus side, there's the giant beehive just underneath the shingles by the deck. An ant colony the size of Manhattan in the back yard. A door lock, here and there, that makes you twist the key with a pair of pliers before it grudgingly opens.

But that's all fixable.

On the plus side, there's the magnificent north window in the kitchen that ripens bananas like no window I've ever seen. Set an ordinary grocery store banana beside it, and in one day's time it's speckled a beautiful brownish-gold, like I've always imagined fruit looks in the tropics where it really feels at home.

And there's the neat little computer inside the thermostat, which can turn the heat and air off and on at selected intervals through the day to save electricity. As soon as I get somebody from NASA to explain it to me, it should be really useful.

There's the upstairs corner window you can see the sunset from, framed by oak leaves—a room that's also radioactive, in the best sense. Hook up an FM radio in it, and you get crystal-clear reception from Tuscaloosa to Gadsden and points beyond.

I like the house so well (once I get past the initial shock of waking up in it, that is) that I keep suspecting there's some kind of catch to all this. A big sinkhole will open up, maybe, and swallow the ground floor. Or some long-ago spirit with a chip on its shoulder will take up residence and start tossing our furniture around at night, like in the movies.

So far, though, the only catch is the mortgage.

But then, what's a little money when you're in love?

Driving Lesson Teaches Dad "How It Is"

He's a good driver, but he's too young to be on the highway yet. That's why you've brought him, this bright Sunday afternoon, to the deserted parking lot of your old grammar school.

Here there's a half-acre of good ground and a circular driveway he can navigate until (wishful thinking, on your part) he gets tired enough to come home.

Being a father, you show him the limits, first—don't go near the blacktop road or get too close to the building. You point out a ditch he should avoid, one a little hidden by its dry grass so that you don't notice how deep it is until you're right on top of it. You show him a patch of loose gravel, and demonstrate how it can make a car slide or spin if you hit it too fast.

And that's it. You get out, he moves to the driver's seat. You squeeze his shoulder once before you shut the door, and then you go sit on a grassy bank to watch.

He rolls up the windows, turns the air conditioner and the radio both to very high settings, gently eases the shift level into DRIVE and he's off—his head nodding in time to a song you can't hear.

And while the small blue station wagon circles the school grounds with slow precision—forward, reverse, forward, parking parallel at a spot on the curb, forward again, reverse, circling, stopping, forward again—you have all the world's time to look at the building where you spent six years of your life, a quarter century ago.

The view has changed. You imagine yourself looking out the windows of Miss Kelley's second-grade room, and you see a new brick house across the road where there once were pine trees and honeysuckle.

At least the old water tower still stands—just to the south, along the road that goes to the high school. But the giant square marker that moved up and down its side, going forever between EMPTY and FULL, appears rusted into place now.

You're amazed at how small all distances have become. The dirt playground that seemed vast enough to get lost in is only a good stone's-throw wide, now. When the principal or one of the teachers would drive over to the high school, then, for a meeting, you'd imagine it as a wilderness safari to the very seat of government. Now it's half a mile, maybe less.

Home seemed an infinite distance away, and that was doubled when you were sick and waiting for a ride there. Two miles? Three? You realize you could run home, now, from this spot, and not even be out of breath.

To the north is the cemetery. It seems larger than it once did. You start counting, in your mind, how many of the stones have the names of your kinfolk on them, and you decide to think of something else.

You think, instead, of the small blue car in the distance, being driven with exquisite care by someone with your name, who's singing a song you don't know the name of. Clouds pass over, a jaybird cries out from a grove of trees.

And you think: So this is how it is.

HOW OLD DOES A FOGEY HAVE TO BE?

How much age is "middle" age?

Forty? Forty-five? Fifty?

Or do they decide on a case-by-case basis, the same way you apply for food stamps or admission to medical school?

I'm a good bit shy of forty, yet, but I have the strangest feeling I'm middle-aged, if you take the definition literally.

Take my hair.

People with long hair take one look at my middle-of-the-ear length and chalk me up as an establishment type, not to be trusted. They probably suspect I voted for Ronald Reagan and own mutual funds. (They're half right.)

Meanwhile, bankers and other short-haired, pinstripe folks on the fast career track take note of my beard and size me up as a liberal. They probably suspect I vote the Democratic ticket and use drugs. (*They're* half right, too.)

And speaking of "middle," let's talk money.

Probably half the wage-earners in the country begrudge me the paycheck I take home every week. I'm making too much money, they feel sure, and have my foot solidly on the neck of the working class.

(Maybe I shouldn't have invested in new gaskets for our garden hose or blown eight dollars on a miraculous device that turns our porch light on at dusk, off at sunup—a complicated sequence of events I could never keep straight in my mind, manually.)

Meanwhile the wealthy people of the world—the corporation owners, the rock stars, and the one or two stockbrokers who still have jobs—feel extremely sorry for me and can't imagine how I survive on what I make.

(Which reminds me of the story about the woman who was getting counsel from a financial advisor: "Live within my *income?*" she repeated, incredulous. "It's all I can do to live within my *credit!*")

Or more to the point, take the somber subject of age.

Young people take one glance and consider me an old fogey—in league with their parents or, more likely, grandparents. Someone who, in brief, wants to return America to the dark ages when songs had words that made sense and when you had to at least contemplate being in love with somebody before you hauled your suitcases over and forwarded your mail.

Old people, on the other hand, consider me a mere babe in the woods—someone who has not paid his dues and doesn't yet grasp how the world works. I can assure them, though, that the best English teacher who ever lived, Pearl Huffman, boiled the world down for me at an early age: "You're the one who makes your bed," she advised us, "and you're the one who's got to lie in it."

Amen. I've got that. I've *got* that.

Old people call me a "boy," which is heartening until I remember that a former neighbor of ours regularly shook his head over the immature carryings-on of his son-in-law. "That boy . . . I declare," he would say, "You can't tell that boy nothing."

"That boy" is seventy-five years old.

I strongly suspect I am into middle age.

My reaction to that fact reminds me of the wonderful scene in the new Martin Sheen movie where he encounters the ghost of his father, whose funeral he's just attended.

"What did it feel like?" Sheen asks the old man's ghost. "Dying, I mean."

The old man shrugs his shoulders. "I didn't care for it," he says.

I feel the same way about approaching middle age. Except that it sure beats the alternative.

And at least nobody can accuse me of going to extremes.

3

On the Road

There's Just Something about a Train

TUSCALOOSA, Ala.—The green woods go rushing past the windows of the railroad car, a blur of dogwood and maple and pine and sunlight, near enough to touch. It feels like we're sitting still, and Birmingham is speeding toward us on a conveyor belt of green leaves.

Down the aisle, a woman with white hair tied in a black ribbon sits doing needlepoint without a sound, her eyes dreaming. Black thread and white, black and white, black and white . . .

"This is good," says Donovan, beside me. "No red lights." He peers through the wide-angle lens on his camera as if to make sure there aren't any red lights he's overlooked. When you're eight years old and have a world of things to do in a hurry, escaping the nuisance of red lights is nothing to sneeze it.

This Sunday is our first train ride, ever.

And it *is* good.

The first leg of our trip—Birmingham to Tuscaloosa, this morning—was on a train that originated in New York City, bound for New Orleans. People throughout the half-filled cars were sprawled in different stages of sleep and exhaustion. There was a scattering of thick coats on the seats beside them. It was hard to imagine a cold place in the world, on a hot Sunday on an Alabama rail through a tunnel of Alabama trees.

Occasionally, a clearing in the woods showed a small church covered with white shingles, surrounded by a bare dirt yard. But the train windows were shut, to keep the air-conditioning inside, and we were going past too quickly to do anything but imagine the sounds of loud singing and good preaching coming from inside. At one church, three little girls, all alone, danced circles in the yard—having escaped from the drone of the service, we guessed, on the pretext of visiting the faraway outhouse beyond the yellow dirt at the woods' edge.

The Tuscaloosa train station was in a lonesome-looking part of town, between a deserted taxi office and a deserted service station.

In the hours before the next train came to take us back to Birmingham, we had time to stroll the sidewalks under a cool forest of hedge bushes hiding old houses that looked as if nobody had lived in them for twenty years. But there were cars in the driveways and curtains on the windows, and the slight noontime breezes made their doors waft open and shut by inches, on their hinges, the only sound in the day.

We found a Beauty Shop with an unbeautiful signboard in front of its unbeautiful building, crumbling and grown up in weeds. Donovan took a picture of it for his scrapbook and wondered aloud what an Ugly Shop must look like.

The empty service station had been visited by nighttime artists with cans of blue spray paint who decorated its cement block walls with big outrageous cartoon faces. We made each other's picture in front of the faces, trying our best to look like them.

And now we're on the way back, through the same tunnel of green we came down on, and everything's quiet except the fizzing of our two glasses of ginger ale and the conversation of two black men near the front of the train car. Their voices rise and fall as comfortingly as the sound of crickets in a shade.

"You used to work there? Did? I worked the same train . . ."

"Lord, I do love to ride a train . . ."

Once you begin loving a train, you never again wonder why so many people have written songs about them. You sit safe and silent while the green woods roar by, and the majesty of it, the feeling of power and humbleness all mixed together, is so strong that you're moved to tell somebody about it. Or to sing.

The Wabash Cannonball. The Orange Blossom Special. City of New Orleans. The Fireball Mail. Train Forty-Five.

The two black men are laughing softly now, at a joke one has told about the strength and speed of some long-ago engine.

"Lord, Lord, yes . . ." one laughs.

Lord, yes.

Watching the Summer Towns Take Off Their Makeup

PORT ST. JOE, Fla.—We wandered through here once at about three o'clock in the morning, sleepy and car weary and without a motel reservation in the very peak of summer when the Gulf Coast was wall-to-wall with vacationers.

Sleep, please. At any price.

Port St. Joe took us in, at a reasonable rate, and the motel owner even pretended he didn't mind getting out of his pajamas and into work clothes to give us a room, at that odd hour.

Now we're back again. Looking, I suppose, for the tail-end of summer along a stretch of beach highway that seems as familiar as the face of an old friend. Ever since I was a kid, my mind has pictured summer as going south when it leaves Walker County. And somehow, this time of year, I always feel like following summer southward, a pretend way of making it stay a little longer, the way a higher-powered jet can chase a sunset across the continent through different time zones.

But this time we're a little too late.

The weather is perfect for sunning. There's a gentle breeze, a blue sky as solid as slate, temperatures that are comfortable even in the heat of the day. The water is so clear, pierced by all these shafts of sun, that you can stand in the dry sand and watch gray crabs with turquoise-colored markings scurry across the sea bottom. Far, far out.

The whole coast is into autumn now, with all its might.

And that fact is apparent to the people who live in this string of towns across the water's edge, people who "summer" here year-round and who batten down their property and their willpower annually against the onslaught of fun-hunting visitors, in much the same way—at least with the hope of some cash to be made—that they secure themselves, at other times of the year, against the fiercest of hurricanes.

Spend a little time at a gas station, a grocery store, or a seafood café just a stone's throw from a boat dock, and you realize that folks' moods resemble, more than anything, the atmosphere backstage among a crowd of actors when the last performance is over and the greasepaint is wiped clean. They breathe freely, slowly. They celebrate by stretching their feet out and looking at the colors in the sky.

They tell jokes. Jokes about unlucky fishermen. About the pope. About Bear Bryant. And they take Alabama's gridiron thrashing in stride, the same way they take a bad-luck day out on the water when the shrimp and lobster seem to have disappeared and the nets are no problem, doggone it, to hoist into the boat. That's life.

Travel this stretch of highway at night, and you see that there's nowhere near the stretch of neon that blazed out from the roadsides a few months ago.

Stores, cafes, marinas are boarded, padlocked. Billboards are plastered with a cornerways slogan, "Closed Till Spring" or "Have A Nice Winter" or "Away Till Next Season."

"Season," of course, meaning the time of year we come, usually. We, the fun-hunters who look on it all like a big neon playground, forgetting that it's someone's home.

But they forgive us, I think. Every year.

And now that we're here, enjoying the beach at its most beautiful and savoring the soft, slow mood of whole towns letting their hair down, I believe we're hooked.

We'll be back, of course, when the crowds descend here again and the sun fries the top of your head and the nighttime brings traffic jams and the biggest forest of neon and saltwater foam you can imagine. Because there's nothing quite like that time.

But I hope we'll chase summer's tail-end to here again, next year. And watch it disappear. And share the moment with some very fine folks and some shrimp and red snapper that taste as though they've been cooked slowly, lovingly, by someone who likes to watch the colors of the sky.

Early Morning Answering Machine a Ray of Sunshine

LOUISVILLE, Ky.—When a person is far from home and has a whole long list of buildings waiting to be photographed as soon as the first bright-yellow wash of sun hits them, a person needs to wake up at 4:00 a.m. or so and stare out past his own lonesome reflection in the hotel window, trying to tell whether rainstorm, tornado, or blessed sunshine is on the way.

I do, anyhow.

I sat in the bed drinking coffee, polishing camera lenses, and double-checking light meters to make sure everything was ready for the frantic few hours when the sunlight's right.

When you *hope* it will be right.

I checked the phone directory to see if Louisville had a Dial-A-Weather-Report, and that's when I got curious.

I didn't see a weather number but, instead, a long list that included Dial-An-Opera, Dial-A-Story, Dial-A-Poem, Dial-A-Prayer, Dial-A-Sermon, Dial-An-Inspiration . . .

The opera was nice. Not an opera, really, but about two minutes' worth of a song from one, which ended with an advertisement for opera tickets.

Dial-A-Poem wouldn't answer. The Dial-A-Story turned out to be a bored-sounding voice telling a supposed children's tale about rabbits and gardens, the moral of which was that everybody should be good and go to church, or else. I didn't see the connection. But then, it was pretty early in the morning.

The man with the sermon sounded as sleepy as me, and the man with the prayer sounded tireder than both of us put together.

I looked out the black window and tried to imagine where this man was, right then, whose voice was saying the same things over and over on a small recorder hooked to a phone somewhere. Was he asleep, or was he staring out a black window of his own, trying to imagine what stranger was listening to his canned voice praying on some phone?

"Lo o o o-r-r-d," the preacher was saying, "let us not be weary . . ." He sounded as if he was weary of praying into a microphone, and maybe weary of life in general.

By the time I took a shower and another bitter dose of coffee, the sky outside was beginning to lighten up—first gray, then a beautiful golden color, and it was obvious no clouds were in sight. All of my 4:00 a.m. pacing had been for nothing.

I started to go downstairs for breakfast, but just to complete the list I called the "inspiration" number. It was a woman's voice, one who sounded excited about living and about the chance to talk to strangers by telephone just as though they were friends. She didn't try to sound holy or mysterious, even when she quoted scripture.

She talked about the problems life deals us sometimes, about the worrying we do and how useless it is.

Most worry comes, she said, from trying to be responsible for more than one day at a time. And that all we can do is our best, and that things will be okay.

Approach each day as if it's a broad, blue sky, just waiting on you, she said. And pretend you've got a brand-new, God-given pair of wings for that particular day, because you do. And move through the day like you've got a right to be there, a right to be limitlessly happy, because you do.

She said she was glad I called, and the recording hummed to a stop.

I was glad, too.

As the cool air of the street hit me that morning, in front of the building, air that smelled suddenly like flowers, I wished there'd been some way to say a thank-you to the machine, deep in the basement of some locked church, no doubt.

Thanks, ma'am. For reminding us all of the wings.

Please don't get weary.

THANK GOODNESS FOR ARTISTS LIKE MR. MILES

PULASKI, Ga.—I should have been suspicious when the gas we bought on the interstate was unusually cheap, but I hate to pass up a bargain.

A few miles down the road, our Chevrolet's old six-cylinder started coughing really bad. When the car slowed down to 20 mph with the gas pedal full to the floor, Donovan and I knew we had problems. Trash in the fuel line, probably.

It was a Saturday, the sun was getting orange in the west, we had hundreds of miles to go before we reached Jekyll Island, our weekend vacation spot, and a look at the road map told us we were a finger's length away (that's many a mile) from Atlanta or any other big city. I pictured my lonesome old toolbox, back home, sitting on the basement steps where I'd left it.

At the next exit we chugged off in search of a mechanic—preferably one with a shelf full of shiny new fuel filters for old-model Chevrolets. Seven miles later, we found that the "gas station" the signboards had advertised was actually a neat white grocery store with two gas pumps out front. No mechanic.

We despaired of being outside Pulaski by bedtime, much less on an island in the Atlantic Ocean.

"But, now, Mr. Miles is a mechanic," the store's proprietor told us. "He lives across the road, there." She pointed through the window toward a white house with some people sitting on the porch watching the sun go down.

We thanked her and chugged across the blacktop into Mr. Miles' driveway, feeling a little guilty about interrupting his quiet Saturday evening with his family.

"Sure," Mr. Miles said. "I'll take a look at it." He was a tanned, wiry man, who looked about fifty years old. He had a white gauze patch behind one lens of his glasses, as if something had injured his eye not long ago. "Pull your car around here; I'll get my tools."

He probed under the hood with two pairs of vise-grip pliers long enough to loosen a stubborn cross-threaded fitting and, finally, extracted an evil-looking button of steel and cloth that was the fuel filter. He tried unsuccessfully to puff some air through it and pronounced our diagnosis correct.

"It's stopped up tighter than Dick's hatband," he said, shaking his head. "Trouble is, I don't have a new one, and all the parts stores are closed by now. Best thing's just to take the bad filter out. The trash'll go on into your carburetor. Won't hurt anything, until you can get a new filter."

He reassembled the fitting, and I cranked the engine. It was good as new. Then suddenly he said, "Whoa, whoa, *whoa,*" and asked me to come look at the small stream of gasoline spurting from the connection. "Hmmm," he said. "Threads stripped worse than I thought."

He went into his house, came back with a spool of sewing thread, and wound it into the grooves of the fuel line. He reattached it with pliers. It didn't leak any more.

"What happened to the hose that's supposed to go over here?" he asked, pointing to another part of the engine. I told him I didn't recall ever seeing a hose there.

"But it's pulling cold air down on your points," he said. "Surely it's making it run rougher. Wait. Wait just a minute . . ." He went to his car trunk and came back with a short length of hose that connected the two bare holes. I cranked the car again. It ran smoother than it had since the Bicentennial year, when it was bought.

He told me our Chevrolet had several more good years left in it. He showed me a '64 Chrysler sitting beside his house, one he'd paid $25 for and rebuilt after its owner wrapped it around a utility pole.

"Thing runs slicker than a meat-skin, now," he said, with obvious pride. "And that air conditioner—why, it's colder than you can stand to sit behind."

I thanked him for getting us headed east again; now we could make the Atlantic Ocean by bedtime, easy.

"How much do we owe you?" I asked.

"Well, sir," he said, as if it were a minor detail, "just whatever you think's right."

I looked at the ten and the twenty and the credit card in my billfold and thought hard. I handed him the ten. "Ten be OK? Or fifteen, maybe?"

He glared at me. "I couldn't do that," he said, glancing down at the ground. I felt I'd hurt his feelings by setting too low a price on his craftsmanship.

"Well," I said, "how about . . ."

He took the ten I offered, reached in his pocket, and gave me back a five. "There," he said. "That's about right."

It took a few seconds to dawn on me what he meant.

"That's not fair," I said. "A service station would have charged me twenty or twent-five, at least, for what you did."

He looked me in the eye. "They're out to take your money," he said. "I ain't."

I told him if he was ever passing through our part of Alabama we'd sure return the favor. I shook his hand, which was warm as a motor and had as many ridges as a good pair of vise-grips.

"Much obliged," I told him. The yard was darkening into evening. I wanted to ask him how many miles he reckoned has passed through his hands, how many engines he'd healed on Saturdays alone, with the sun going down. But I felt I'd be prying.

I aimed the Chevrolet toward the ocean and let him get back to his family, thinking that if a writer of novels had invented a mechanic this good and named him Miles, some editor somewhere would say that was too obvious a gimmick. Another name, surely, would be more believable.

Some part of me gave thanks that there are artists still alive and thriving in the most unlikely places, unhired by any corporation with a high-gloss sign whose main aim is to take your money and never give in return a single ounce of pride or inventiveness, much less a life time of it—corporations with youngsters on their payrolls who have never made any automobile, much less a wrecked antique one, run as smooth as a meat-skin.

Good to know you, Mr. Miles. And God bless you.

Aerial View Puts Ancient History in Perspective

TAZEWELL, Tenn.—The cabin of this small plane is as warm as our kitchen was before sunup, this morning, when I left for the Birmingham airport. Groggy from too little sleep, I'd hoped to catch a nap of sorts while we flew. But I see there's no chance of that, now.

Because somewhere near the Tennessee line the sun raised its head and threw a gold, slanting light across the tail end of the Smoky Mountains. The farther north we've come the thicker and whiter the carpet of snow has gotten until, now, the mountains stretching all four directions like pieces of white velvet lying in wrinkles where they've fallen.

Watching it pass slowly underneath is so much like a dream, and a good one, that I can't bring myself to shut my eyes and settle for a real dream—it would likely be quick and shabby and citified and otherwise confused, the way dreams are when you're turning over in bed one last time before starting a hard day's work. Dreams, by that hour, know they're on borrowed time.

So I've been noticing for an hour now how many different shapes the ground can take, no two alike, once the distractions of roads and wires and roofs are blotted out by something soft and white.

This place looks to be a countryside of small farms, slanted facets of ground cut into hillsides so steep you'd probably have to stand spraddle-legged to keep upright. No tire tracks, yet, have defined the white creases where the roadways must be.

The angle of the sun, by now, is giving the mountains of snow the look of sequins, glinting in rainbow colors too bright to look at directly without them leaving their painful purple after-shapes on your eyeballs.

Only two things now and then break up the pattern of glistening white and silver. A pond or lake that the wind is whipping into a frenzy looks to be on fire, down in its black depths, with the blue flame of the sun. And there are odd black tracings in some of the pastures, almost like pencil sketches with a dot at the end of each line.

I've finally figured out that the spider-web-looking lines are the footpaths cattle have taken from the places they slept, and the dots at the end of the lines are where the cattle stand now, not moving, as if they're now charged with making their lives in this new white world, somehow, without the old one of brown dirt and grass they went to sleep in, the night before. No two of their paths are alike.

It all brings to mind something I read in a magazine, a few days back, about the giant pictures the Aztec Indians dug and painted into their soil hundreds or thousands of years ago. Nobody knew the pictures existed until the first fledgling airplanes began crisscrossing that part of the world. The pilots were shocked to see detailed drawings of a spider, a monkey, a sun, and numerous geometric shapes they couldn't ascribe a meaning to.

The pictures have led the more excitable of the experts to speculate that the Aztecs had their own airplanes, centuries before the rest of the world. Or that they cruised around their countryside in hot-air balloons, making sketches of the pictures they would later lay out, acres wide, down on the ground. Or, most spectacular of all, that the pictures were actually landing strips for flying saucers, and that the Aztecs didn't know what they were constructing, but only followed the directions given to them by spacemen.

All of that seems a bit hard to swallow, from up here, this early in the morning on this beautiful a day.

From here, it's much easier to suspect a simpler explanation. How improbable it would be for men without trains or airplanes or telegraphs or radios to look up into the silent sky at times, marveling at the patterns and colors that the clouds and sun make, and wonder . . . what if . . . *just suppose* . . . that there's someone out in those reaches somewhere, even though they can't be seen from the ground, and that someone is watching the broad spread of land from his small perch of sky, just like we're watching the whole broad sky from the narrow patch of dirt.

Wouldn't it be a good idea to show that person some shapes of things we see, down here, and see if he responds by showing us things too far away for us to see? Wouldn't that person up there enjoy it? Wouldn't he feel privileged? Seems so. To see hundreds of miles with one sweep of the eye. Imagine.

And they weren't wrong. Sure enough, it's a joy. A privilege.

A Storybook Island Waits for the Thunder

DAUPHIN ISLAND, Ala.—When the hurricane swept across the Gulf here, last year, it bit clean through the big iron bridge that connected the island with the Alabama coast near Theodore.

So today at dawn, bound for the island, we found that our road came to a sudden end at the water's edge. We parked near a hill of sand and got out to wade a while in the foam made silver-colored by the sunrise, until the small boat came that would take us to Dauphin.

It's barely a twenty-minute ride, we found—a ride with sunshine and salt spray in our faces, as the boy at the boat's helm took it hopping and jigging over the choppy sea, steering us around the lonely bridge pilings that had been stripped clean as chicken bones by the long-ago holocaust of wind.

We weren't there to write about the bridge, but about a young marine biologist who works on the island at a government experiment station, tracking down a cholera-like disease carried by shellfish.

The question of the bridge's future hung so thickly in the air, though, that we couldn't help asking about it. At that moment, a federal judge in a faraway oak-paneled room sat deciding the island's fate. A court suit had halted the $23-million rebuilding project, claiming that heavy traffic would damage the island's delicate ecological balance.

The boy piloting the boat didn't have much to say on the matter. He quickly changed the subject to a low line of black clouds stirring on the horizon:

"Some rain, there," he said. And then he was silent.

The biologist, Miles Moates, had prepared us for the island people's tight-lipped ways as we sat with him and his wife Debbie the night before, over platters of fried shrimp and coleslaw.

"It's like . . ." Miles began, and then thought hard before he finished. "It's like they're in a different world. The islanders, I mean. If they're real quiet, don't take it personally. They just don't care much for talking to anybody they don't know."

He prophesied right. All day, people who had been unfailingly courteous when talking about the weather or the tides, or about how self-sufficient a man or a woman has to be when the nearest town has no road to it, regressed to shrugs and sighs when the subject of the bridge came up.

"I can take it," one man said. Just as he spoke, a small boy, shirtless and bronze-backed, sped out of the scrub pines on a bicycle with a black hound in happy pursuit.

"Really, I can take it either way. I'm ready for whatever they say."

He didn't hide the fact that his teeth were clenched ever so slightly as he spoke, like someone braced for a hard blow.

Another of the few who voiced an opinion said that the question had been decided when the first bridge was built. "The damage has already been done," he said. "What's a little more?"

The sky stayed brilliantly blue for most of the morning, but the line of storm clouds that had shown themselves as we made the crossing kept stirring along the horizon—distant thunder, a cool breeze threatening rain.

When we took a break from our interviewing and picture-taking to sit in the shade with Miles and sip a Coke, he told us that he hasn't always lived on the mainland where he does now—a brick house in a subdivision.

Just after he and Debbie married, they lived on the island. In a cabin right at the water's edge. It was, he remembers, like being in a dream. "I could walk right out the front door and catch some fish. Cook them for breakfast. It was something, I tell you."

But the dream deteriorated, over the years. The cabin was near a public picnic area. And as tourist traffic increased, so did the problems. One day Miles' and Debbie's golden cocker spaniel disappeared into a friendly car. They never saw him again.

Miles said he can see both sides of the bridge question and admits there's no perfect solution. He suspects the bridge will get the go-ahead, anyway.

Later in the day, an older man who lives on the mainland but works on the island sat talking to us concerning his own two-mindedness about the bridge.

"Years ago, none of this was here," he said, motioning with disdain to a cluster of new houses on a jutting finger of land across the beach. As we listened, the sky finally whitened above us, and the long-delayed storm brought a refreshing shower of rain.

"You see, the easier it is to get here, the faster this kind of building will happen. Just think, five years after the bridge is reopened. Ten years . . ."

If you looked closely at his eyes, you could see images of motels and neon and hamburger stands dancing sadly in his head.

Then it was time for us to go. The boat was waiting, with its young silent helmsman, to take us back to the world.

I was back at home the next Monday, eating breakfast, when I heard the news on the radio.

Yes, the judge had said. Build the bridge.

I could imagine the islanders waking up to the same news, as clouds sped by and the wind tossed the palm fronds and the rising sun turned the surf silver-colored just beyond their porch steps.

All too soon, they'll be hearing a very different kind of thunder.

One that will bring a lot more than rain.

GOSPEL SINGING SITE IS A PIECE OF HEAVEN

HOMINY VALLEY, N.C.—When you drive into town here, you don't see a big sign saying "Gospel Singing Capital of the South," but that's probably because the folks are too modest for that.

Hominy Valley is in the edge of the Great Smokies. When we spread our quilt on this grassy hillside a couple of hours ago, just after sunset, there was a soft blue haze of mountains on every side, stretching as far as you could see.

Since it's gotten dark, though, the small covered stage just downhill is the main attraction. Several quartets have already been up and, after a short break for the crowd to stretch their legs and go to the concession stand, all the groups are getting ready to go another round.

These are not your typical quartets. No sequins on their clothes, no loud razzle-dazzle. Just good harmony singing that occasionally makes the hair on your neck rise up. Which is my own benchmark for measuring good gospel.

Doyle Lawson and his group Quicksilver are on stage now. Their biggest crowd-pleaser so far was *Jesus Gave Me Water, And It Was Not From the Well.* That one had several of the younger folks on their feet, clapping and singing along. The older people, many of them with canes and walkers propped beside their chairs, raise their hands into the air from time to time, and some of them wipe their eyes.

Jesus gave me water
He gave me that living water
Jesus gave me water
And it was not from the well . . .

People here take their gospel singing seriously.

Off to the side, for instance, there are two girls about eight years old who look to be buddies. Right now they're catching lightning bugs, but while they stalk them they're singing softly in time to the music. Watch their lips, and you realize they know all the words to all the great old-time songs. Eight years old.

Just uphill, under a canvas tent, the local rescue squad is selling barbecue and cold drinks and coffee and business has been good. If you want slaw with your barbecue, though, you'll have to wait a few minutes. They ran out of slaw, and the ambulance is gone to get some more.

Quicksilver is singing:

My rock
My shield
My Jesus is real
I can feel him deep within
My so-o-o-o-oul . . .

The hometown favorites, though, are probably the Primitive Quartet.

The group, from here in Hominy Valley, is host for the yearly singings in this gently sloping field that looks to have been a pasture at one time.

The members of the Primitive Quartet are scattered at the edge of the crowd, waiting to go on next, and talking quietly with fans who spot them and wander over to shake hands or, more often, hug their necks. One of the members has been gradually working uphill toward the restrooms for nearly a half hour now, but he's been hugged so many times he's only made it half the way.

The night is as clear as crystal. Stars sparkle overhead, a lot more of them than you see in a city.

This trip, we've decided to skip the motels. Our tent is already pitched, about ten miles west of here, beside a big lake with brown and white ducks in it. In the morning the sun will come up across the lake, and I'll be awakened by an impatient duck in search of breakfast who will nab my big toe through the fabric of the tent.

Right now, though, there's a lot more singing still to go. And nobody, young or old, looks to be in a hurry to leave.

Quicksilver is singing:

I'll have a new body,
Praise the Lord
I'll have a new life . . .

It sounds mighty good. But nobody seems in any hurry to lay claim to it, just yet.

Because tonight, in Hominy Valley, this body—and this life—will do just fine, thank you.

4

Famous People

George Jones Is Better, and He Sends His Love

It was very late one night, back during the winter, and several of us were sitting in the living room of a friend's house, way over in Arkansas, listening to records—Bluegrass and old-time country—when the subject of George Jones came up.

We agreed, with no abstainers, that no singer, living or dead, can send chills up your back with a sad country song the way George can. Singers from far and near poke gentle fun at his voice from time to time, with their impersonations, but there's a deep reverence for him, even in the fun. A legend is a legend.

We sipped our hot tea and nodded assent. The album on the stereo ended and the needle clicked off to silence, leaving only a barely heard electrical hum, the amplifier straining to pull music from the air when there was none left.

A friend broke the quiet. "You know, some days I'll be working or eating lunch or whatever, and all of a sudden I'll think, 'I wonder what George Jones is doing right now?'" He stared at the window, the dark. "I worry about him. I really do. I hate to see him have so much trouble. I worry like he was somebody I know, like he was one of the family. Isn't that strange? I mean, considering how many other things there are to worry about?"

Then, one by one, we all admitted that we worried about George too, at odd times of the day or night, and how we hated to see his life keep getting messed up by the drinking and the pills, how we wished there was something we could do to help.

None of us spoke for a minute, then, until finally somebody said, "Lord, God, that man can sing." That was the truth, we all allowed, and then agreed (no abstainers, again) that it was long past bedtime.

By the time George Jones' band came onstage at Boutwell Auditorium Friday night, it was plain that this was no fancy-chitchat, polite-applause crowd. This was blue jeans and boots and overalls, people who work for a living.

An hour before, when the girl singer with the warmup band had lit into "I'm proud to be a coal miner's daughter . . ." there were scattered rebel yells as far away as the men's room, where I happened to be at the time. And when the members of the warm-up band were introduced, they told where each of them was from, and the fellow from Walker County got the biggest applause of all.

The Jones Boys came out next and did a few songs without George ("It's good to be in Birmingham . . . finally," one of them joked, referring to George's habit of having to cancel shows at the last minute sometimes; "Third time's the charm, I guess," and that made the crowd laugh), but the clapping and stomping and shouts of "Where's George?" finally brought him out. He looks smaller and more fragile than his voice would make you believe. His big guitar makes him look, except for the lines in his face, almost like a mischievous youngster who's picked up something belonging to grownups.

"The bars . . . are all closed . . ." he sings. "It's four in . . the mornin' . . . I must have shut 'em all down . . . from the shape that I'm in . . ." And it becomes plain that even if his show ended right then with the last note of that song, not many folks would have the nerve to ask for their money back.

When he comes to the line, "With the blood from my body, I could start my own still," he grins a little and tucks his head down. Underneath the styled sweep of gray hair, his pointed face is evangelist and con man and repentant little boy, all rolled into one. Despite the sore throat he's apologized for twice, tonight, it's possible that the "little ol' short-legged guitar picker," as he describes himself, is actually what the emcee had claimed he is—"Ladies and gentlemen, the greatest country singer of all time . . ."

His voice can wring more pain from a single note than your ears can believe, on first hearing; can bend the same tone twelve ways to accommodate all the hurting in it, and then polish all the broken edges smooth again with a whispery grace-note that tells you he'll keep trying, anyway, to find the right kind of woman and the right kind of life.

Tonight he sings a song about Jesus, then another one about a woman who ". . . don't shine for the rest of the world; she's too busy shining on me . . ." He begins "He Stopped Loving Her Today" and the crowd is on its feet, shouting and applauding, even though his amazing voice goes away to thin air for a word or two, making the harmony singer jump in nervously to fill the gap.

The good part about listening to a legend with a sore throat is that your memory supplies whatever's missing; you can tell it by watching the faces in the dark auditorium, silently mouthing the words they know by heart, some of the people with their eyes closed to see the lonesomeness better.

When the song is through, and the applause bursts up and then goes on and on, a river of it, George tells them, "Thank y'all, really. Thank y'all so much. I know y'all love me, or you wouldn't be here.

"And I hope you know . . . I hope you know I love *y'all* or I wouldn't be here."

On my way out I stood in a long line to buy a T-shirt as a souvenir. It has a picture of George grinning on the front and, on the back, the slogan I SAW NO-SHOW JONES.

I'm not much for writing letters to folks. Seems like there's not much of that done, anymore. But the one thing that obligates you to write a letter is when you have some news from a member of the family that others would be comforted to hear. "I have heard from Aunt Geneva," you might say, "and she's out of the hospital, up there in Tennessee, and is eating solid food now . . ."

I've started a letter to the folks who were at the house in Arkansas, that night, to tell them that I've heard from George. To tell them that he seems to be doing much better than he was, last winter. And to tell them that, Lord God, he can still sing a song.

And that he sends his love.

But Would Michael Jackson Make a Good Vice President?

Mr. Short?" said the long-distance voice on the telephone. "This is *USA Today*, in Washington."

I listened for a second to the faint hissing sound a long-distance phone line makes and tried to guess what *USA Today* might want. I was moderately sure I hadn't forgotten to pay for my subscription, seeing as I don't subscribe.

"We need you to write a story for us," the voice said.

My mind hummed with the possibilities. An exclusive talk with Henry Kissinger? Or, better, a meticulously researched feature on the resort areas of Tahiti, with air fare and beachfront hotel paid? Such a grueling task might take weeks, I reasoned.

"What kind of story?" I asked, laying my cards right on the table.

"As you might be aware," the far-off editor said, in a tone that suggested international intrigue, "Michael Jackson is in Birmingham."

"Yes, I heard about that," I said. (It's important to let an editor know, right off, that you occasionally read newspapers.) A Michael Jackson interview is not to be sneezed at, I told myself.

"You've arranged a Michael Jackson interview?" I asked, laying my cards right on the table again.

"Oh, no," the editor said, laying his cards right on the table. "We need a reaction piece. How do people in Birmingham *feel* about Michael Jackson being there? What's happening in the lobby of the hotel where the Jacksons are staying? Things like that."

"Ah," I said. "How soon do you need all this?"

"Could you phone it in by 3:30?" he asked.

I looked at the clock. It was a little after 11:00.

"You mean, 3:00 *today*?" I asked.

"Yep. Can you handle it?"

"Sure," I said, throwing caution to the wind. I hadn't done any reporting on a daily deadline for about eight years, and I missed it. Once every few years. Briefly.

I reached for my reporter's notebook. It wasn't there. Hadn't been for about eight years, come to think of it.

I stopped at a small grocery store near my office and found a notebook small enough to fit in my pocket. It was orange and had a picture of a spotted puppy standing in some tulips. I picked out a new ink pen, too. Might as well do this up right, I figured.

The checkout line at the store was a long one, mostly mothers with babies who occupied themselves by chewing the knees of the grownups in line. (The babies, not the mothers.)

By the time I paid for my notebook and pen it was a quarter till twelve. I suddenly realized that I was going to spend the next three hours chasing teenage girls and asking them what they thought about Michael Jackson, and I was already hungry before I started. I went back into the store for two packs of peanuts and a large Grapico.

I asked the elderly lady who rang up my peanuts and Grapico what she thought about Michael Jackson being in town.

She thought a minute. "Well," she finally said, her jaw clenched, "they keep talking him up, but I don't think he'd make a good vice president."

The lobby of the Hyatt House was full of teenage girls who giggled and chewed their knuckles a lot. Whenever an elevator door opened or a big car pulled up outside, they scattered in its direction like a covey of quail.

I made a note of that fact in my orange notebook.

A middle-aged woman ran into the lobby excitedly, as if she'd just gotten the news. "Are the Jacksons staying in this hotel?" she asked the desk clerk.

"No, ma'am" the clerk answered, wearily, as four bellhops passed by carrying huge shipping cases stenciled GERMAINE, MICHAEL, and TITO on their sides. The woman sighed, disappointed, and left.

I asked everybody in the lobby, one by one, what they thought about Michael Jackson rehearsing in town and whether they planned to see one of his concerts when his show came to Florida. The consensus was that Michael is cute and neat and can sure enough dance, and that they believed they would faint if they actually did see him right then, and that they would go see his show in Florida if they could aggravate their parents enough.

Then I asked everybody *outside* the lobby what they thought about Michael Jackson being in town. I talked to everyone in the area, I think, except a street sweeper up on Eleventh Avenue.

No, scratch that. I *did* talk to him.

He said he had nothing against Michael, but he didn't plan to see one of his concerts because there was too much other good stuff you could do with thirty dollars.

I sat down behind a big potted fern and wrote my story, and then frantically looked for a pay phone that wasn't being used.

I found one. My watch said 3:29.

"I hope you didn't spend a lot of time polishing your story," the long-distance voice said as I started reading the story to him. "We'll probably change it all around, anyway, to fit our style, you know?"

When I finished dictating the story I stuck my notebook in my pocket and went looking for something more substantial to eat than peanuts and a Grapico. On the way, I pondered the events of the day.

I decided that it was fun being back in reporter's harness for a day, and that I might try it again in a few years. And I decided that Michael Jackson is neat and cute and can sure enough dance, though I probably would not have fainted if I'd actually seen him right now.

I don't think he'd make a good vice president, though.

STEPHEN FOSTER'S VISION STILL A SOOTHING OASIS

WHITE SPRINGS, Fla.—A quiet, shallow river runs through the edge of town here. Its banks are sandy. Old oaks hold a dense shade, even at noon.

But there are no fishermen in sight—only a half-dozen black youths, all about ten years old, shirtless, walking barefooted and using branches torn from a sapling to poke in the yellowish-white sand, looking for nothing in particular.

Drive across the old bridge, and you notice the sign:

SUWANEE RIVER.

Before you can say to yourself, "that's odd; the same name as the song . . ." the words and tune have already formed in your mind and you're singing them despite yourself:

Way down upon the Swan-e-e-e River,

Far, far awa-a-a-ay . . .

It's no coincidence, though the real Suwanee has gained a *u* over the century. Pass over the quiet river and, a few blocks nearer downtown White Springs, a small distinguished sign points the way to the Stephen Foster Memorial Museum.

By now, I'm not surprised to run into Stephen Foster anywhere—even here, on a long, slow drive to the seacoast of Georgia. He's been dogging my steps for the last two months. If I had a little stronger belief in psychic phenomena, I would be most thoroughly spooked by this time. His name and his melodies keep meeting me at the oddest hours, around the most unlikely corners.

It began on the first hot night of this past spring, a midnight tribute to the composer on public radio. A woman with a beautiful, mellow voice sang his best tunes, with a single piano for accompaniment, and two scholarly sounding men talked about Foster's life and music.

In the summer of 1980, when the number-one pop song in the nation consists of a female singer whining "talk about it, talk about it, talk about i-i-i-i-t . . ." endlessly, with a melody line as tuneless as a jackhammer, the hundred-year-old music of Stephen Foster is as soothing an oasis as the

Suwanee River itself.

I dream of Jeanie with the light brown hair,
Borne like a vapor on the summer air . . .

Sitting on the wide green lawn of the Foster Memorial, a grouping of light-colored antebellum buildings overhung by huge oaks, it's easy to imagine Foster scribbling on a notepad, humming to himself, with a full moon shining and the odor of magnolias wafting in the air.

It's easy to imagine, but it's far from the truth.

The man who romanticized and immortalized an entire era of the South only visited it a handful of times in his thirty-eight years of life. He lived and wrote mostly in the cold, gritty industrial cities of the North.

Even as a teenager, he wanted to be a serious composer. His family preferred a more stable career for him, though, and helped him get a job as a clerk for a Cincinnati steamship line, where his ledgers were said to be "models of neatness and accuracy." In his free time he began writing songs for the Negro minstrel show, whose popularity was on the upswing in the mid-1800s.

He did it mainly for the resultant paycheck. He asked the publishers of the sheet music to leave his name off, so that such "frivolous" writing wouldn't keep people from taking him seriously as a real songwriter when he eventually made his mark in music. In the meantime, though, he joked with his friends that he intended to become "the greatest writer of minstrel music in the world."

Weep no more, my lady, weep no more today
We will sing one song for the Old Kentucky Home,
For the Old Kentucky Home far away.

It's ironic that the man who wrote two of the most beautiful melodies in all of music, "I Dream of Jeanie" and "Beautiful Dreamer" saw his own dreams mostly crumble. He made lots of money, spent even more, suffered through ill health, alcoholism, and a disastrously mismatched marriage. He died penniless in New York City, from injuries received in a fall, at the age of thirty-eight.

It's probable that even his own imagination couldn't encompass his music's impact on the world. No matter that some of his concert hall numbers' gentility has fallen into disfavor among contemporary souls, or that his mistily romanticized references to happy slaves aren't exactly the anthem of the civil rights movement.

Travelers to Arabia, Africa, Japan, and other far shores have told of awakening to Stephen Foster songs sung in English by workers and housemaids.

Beautiful dreamer, wake unto me

Starlight and dewdrops are waiting for thee . . .

No doubt if he could tour his own memorial museum today, he'd be surprised his "un-serious" music has survived so richly. He probably wouldn't spend much time in the stuffiness of these walls, though, but would walk down to the Suwanee and wait for sunset.

A uniformed guard has come to lock the museum doors for the evening. There's still an hour of daylight left, for a visitor to sit on the lawn and imagine.

Imagine, and wonder what hall or alleyway the next Stephen Foster song will meet me in. I've come to carry his songs in my mind, these weeks, the way my kid self carried a smooth, cool piece of flintrock in a pocket, a soothing thought just to know it's there for the touching.

I don't know it yet, here on the lawn, but four days from now in the heart of bustling Atlanta a record store's discount rack will be displaying a battered album, "Stephen Foster Songs," priced at far less than it's worth.

I'll buy it, immediately, since it's waiting there expressly for me, and the drive home will be more soothing just for having the album lying in the back seat, smooth and cool, there for the touching.

I'll be glad to see it on the record store rack, out of place amid the high walls crammed with disco and metallic rock.

Glad. But not at all surprised.

What Would Joe Namath Give To Be a Nobody?

To judge from all the nervous folks standing around on the darkened stage of Boutwell Auditorium, talking in low murmurs, a tornado might have been on the way—or something equally fearsome.

"When?"

"Any minute now, I heard . . ."

"Somebody said he . . ."

"They've gone to get him. I heard them say somebody's gone to get him . . ."

But the shape that sauntered up out of the dressing-room hallway, wearing a knit shirt and Bermuda shorts, was not an imposing one at all. He shook hands with the newspaper photographers and TV cameramen who were stringing their cords and cables and lights across the edge of the stage, preparing to take the publicity pictures that would appear on a million papers and TV screens the next weekend.

He looked healthy and relaxed, but he dragged a troublesome knee somewhat, and if you hadn't recognized his face instantly from TV and magazines and movies, you might have assumed he was a public relations man who'd hurt his leg jogging. Or maybe a teacher, or a coach of some kind.

"Hi. I'm Joe," he said in a low, half-shy voice, to the first of dozens of onlookers who milled shyly in line to shake hands with him.

"I'm Pam," the girl said.

"I'm Jan," said the girl behind her.

"Hi," said Joe. "I'm Joe."

"My name's Teresa . . ."

"Hi, Teresa. I'm Joe."

"I'm Tom."

"Hi, Tom. Joe."

His voice was soft, but his face screamed "Joe NAMATH!" to anybody who's ever bought shaving cream or watched football or a late-night variety show. If you did a survey of the country's best-known faces, his would have to rate pretty high.

He was in town to star in a play, but this afternoon he took a few hours to pose for uncountable pictures with uncountable people, from co-stars to stage managers to people in the chorus. A lady with a notepad, off to the side, would find out all their hometowns, and a copy of the picture would go out the next day to each of the hometown papers, spreading the news that they were about to appear on the same stage with Joe Namath.

The afternoon passed slowly. Directors directed, managers managed, promoters promoted—all of them eyeing their watches nervously, gently pulling Joe to one side of the stage, then the other, for pictures. *Just one more. Here, Joe. Could you set up next for . . . oh, I'm sorry. I forgot. One more here, then. And you'll need to change clothes for the other . . . and then . . .*

And Joe, at the center of the storm, remained unfailingly polite and unruffled.

And meanwhile the line of well-wishers keep coming.

"I'm Natalie." Blush, blush.

"Hi. I'm Joe."

"I'm David."

"Hi, David. I'm Joe . . ."

It's easy to be cynical about somebody who has parlayed an amazing football career, a handsome face, and an "Aw, shucks" grin into a million-dollar business.

Hard work? Oh, yeah, he works hard. (Snicker, snicker.)

But face to face, the target of the cynicism is a good old down-to-earth Alabama boy—even if he's a transplanted one. And with a hint of a New York accent, at that.

"I tell myself, gol-LEE, Joe, you gotta watch that Northern accent. You're back in Alabama, now, somebody'll get the wrong idea . . .")

"I'm Barbara."

"Hi, Barbara. I'm Joe . . ."

"I'm Carl. And my son will never forgive me if I don't get your autograph while I'm here. Would you? Do you have time? I think I've got something to write on, here . . ."

"Don't let him slip a blank check under there, Joe," a bystander laughs. And Joe laughs, as if he's never heard the joke before.

Watching all the commotion, from the shadows, you have to wonder how big a check Joe Namath would write, if he could, to be able to walk down a sidewalk or eat in a restaurant, for once, without an admiring horde squeezing in close and bringing out their autograph materials and introducing themselves.

"Hey, aren't you JOE NAMATH?"

"Hey . . ."

"Hey . . ."

A long time before Joe Namath was born, a lady who never ventured far from her house was writing poems which she didn't think anybody would care to read. She would probably be as surprised as anybody, today, to find them in English textbooks around the world, and to find actresses portraying her in TV specials and Broadway plays.

Her name was Emily Dickinson, and she wrote a poem that I'll bet Joe can identify with.

Emily didn't even give her poems names, but it's the one that begins:

I'm nobody! Who are you?
Are you nobody too?

And it ends with:

How dreary to be somebody!
How public, like a frog
To tell your name the live-long day
To an admiring bog . . .

Joe, this is Emily.

Emily . . . Joe.

5

Passings

Thelma Sexton: An Extremely Un-Ordinary Woman

All this week I've wracked my brain trying to remember the first time I met Thelma Sexton, but I keep drawing a blank.

Looking back, it seems she was always there, ever since that prehistoric summer—1971, if memory serves me—when, at the tender age of twenty, I lucked into being editor of the biggest weekly newspaper in the state.

Each week we put out either twenty-four or thirty-six pages, and if you've ever had to write enough stuff to fill up even a single newspaper page, you can imagine how busy I was, and how exhilarated. And how scared.

Luckily we had the help of some two dozen "community correspondents," who were badly underpaid for the thankless job of writing weekly columns about what was going on in their area—births, deaths, marriages, who visited who, whose kid made the honor roll. All the things that, in the long haul, probably have more to do with our daily lives than who's running for city council or who's trying to rezone a piece of land.

Thelma was a correspondent, and a good one. She and her husband Bill had a son in the same high school I'd gone to, and they lived on the same fork of the Warrior River where my father and my grandfather grew up, so I was always partial to her, a little, for that reason alone.

Besides, she was one of a small elite group of correspondents (including Kitty Bennett, Fay Bobo, A. J. Lee, and a precious few others) who were a joy to work with because their copy was always well-crafted, always on time, and because they never called to bless me out when their sentences got chopped off in print or a typographical error made someone have "a roach for dinner" instead of "the coach for dinner."

One day Thelma came by the newspaper office and told me she wanted to broaden her column a little. "I want to make it more than just who visited who," she said. She wanted to include some memories about growing up in Kentucky. Some occasional words of inspiration that had meant a lot to her. Good books she'd read. Things like that.

Sure, I told her. Go ahead. And she did. It made for good reading.

After I left the paper in 1975 to work for *The Birmingham News*, I lost touch with Thelma for a long time. Between the move to town, a new job, a two-year-old son, the beginnings of a divorce, another new job, and eventually remarrying, I left several good friendships on hold much longer than I should have.

Then, two years ago, I heard from Thelma again. She's started going to the same church as my grandparents, and one Sunday she sent me a small cutting of a cactus plant to use on my writing desk.

That was the same week, ironically, that I heard she was dying.

I made plans to go see her. And dreaded it. I've never been much good at consoling anybody.

Knowing Thelma, though, I shouldn't have worried. *She* consoled *me*. We laughed and talked and reminisced about the newspaper and had a great afternoon.

She talked about the cancer and her treatments in a factual and dry-eyed way, which was the way she approached everything. The word "self-pity" was not in her vocabulary. She knew her time was running out, she said, so it was important that she live every day the best she knew how, which to her meant being with people she cared about and helping them whenever she could.

In the months to come, she would call me from time to time and recommend a good book she'd just read, or tell me an idea she'd had for an article or a novel or a movie script. She knew she wouldn't have time to follow up on the ideas herself, she said, so if I could make anything of them, I was welcome.

She said she didn't know if the ideas were any good or not. Most of them were so good they gave me goosebumps.

Occasionally, I'd send her copies of articles and stories I was working on to get her reaction. I tried my hand at comedy writing with a short story and sent her a copy. She told me later that she laughed out loud when she read it, a fact that put me on a cloud for days. Her opinion carried a lot of weight with me. A few months later the story won a prize in a contest. Now, when I think of that story, what I'm most proud of is not the small plaque it got but rather the fact that it once made Thelma laugh out loud.

A book that had meant a lot to her, she told me, was one called *Death Be Not Proud*, a father's account of his teenage son's battle with cancer. She wanted to write something like that, she said, because there were so many things about life she hadn't realized until her illness. And wouldn't it be great if somebody somewhere who was going through rough times of their own could get some comfort from what she wrote?

I don't think she got very far on the project, though, because she was too busy with other things. Even when she was in and out of the hospital regularly, she still worked as a phone volunteer for the Crisis Center, listening to people's problems, helping however she could.

There's the temptation, when somebody you care about dies, to make them out better than they really were. But with Thelma, that's not a problem. The reality was enough. I'm sure that in her weaker moments she could be as spiteful and self-centered as the rest of us, but I never saw evidence of it.

When my grandfather called to tell me about the funeral this week, he said, "She was not your ordinary woman." The brevity was characteristic of him—putting into six words what it takes a professional like me several hundred to say less well.

Whenever I sit at my writing desk now, trying against the odds to string together words that mean something, the cactus reminds me of how lucky

I am to have known her. With this past week's warm weather spurring it on, the thing's growing so fast you can almost watch the bright green leaves pop out.

Just this morning, I noticed a new spot of color at the tip of it, different from the green, and when I looked close I saw that the newest sharp spines it's putting out are a brilliant red, almost translucent, the color of an expensive ruby.

And it occurs to me why I've always been partial to cactus plants. They're tough, and they don't draw attention to themselves. But when you least expect it, they're capable of small beautiful acts that remind you how sweet it is just to be alive.

I guess you could say they're Thelma's kind of plant.

EMMETT DAIL: HE'D HELP YOU IF HE COULD

The small church sat in a clearing at the end of a redrock path. Walking inside it from out of the midday heat was a surprise to your face, because the building still held so much coolness from the morning.

Only the casket was inside, no mourners yet. Out the window, you could see the undertaker waiting in the yard under the shade of a big oak. There was no sound anywhere but the quiet ticking that comes from the walls of a building sometimes, from the hidden places, when the days have been hot and dry.

Emmett's nose and forehead showed just above the sides of the metal box. His face was the smooth brown color of cocoa in a cup, just like it always was, and his profile had a kingly bearing to it, like always. He looked as if he might have had some French in his ancestry, way back.

He always had a knack for cooking, and he could set a fine table. Many a family, around where we lived, would hire him to come help when they had more guests coming than they could handle alone.

Emmett was a good nurse, too, from what I knew. He spent a lot of his time with sick and dying people, back before our hospitals and nursing homes and mortuaries took over so many of the functions neighbors used to do for each other. When you went to see someone who had died at home, Emmett would be the one to lift up the white cotton cloth that was over them. Then he would kind of turn his eyes away so that you could look privately at their face for as long as you wanted.

Emmett lived to be about eighty, I think. Maybe in all those years death had lost some of its strangeness to him. Maybe that was why he looked so peaceful that afternoon, in the coolness of the church just a couple of hillsides away from where he had lived.

Just a few months ago, Emmett sat on the side of his bed in a Jasper nursing home and shook hands with my grandparents who'd come to visit him.

"Come closer," he said to my grandfather, and when he'd leaned forward Emmett said again to him, "Closer," as if he wanted to whisper a secret. Then Emmett reached up and hugged him, holding him for several seconds without saying anything.

Then, a few days ago, the shiny car with the Michigan license plates pulled into their driveway. "You remember me, don't you?" the young man said, and my grandfather recognized him as a nephew or cousin of Emmett's who came to Alabama to visit from time to time.

"I was hoping you'd brought Emmett to see us," my grandfather said, but the man just looked past him, down at the grass of the yard, like there were lots of things on his mind.

"That's what I came to tell you about," he said.

The church slowly began to fill up. A woman handed out cardboard fans, and a young girl with braided hair gave out copies of a printed program listing the songs and scripture that would be used for the funeral. The program had Emmett's name on the front in bold letters, MR. EMMETT DAIL, and for some reason it looked strange, written out like that, after just hearing it spoken for so many years.

A choir of a half-dozen women sang some songs, and then one of them sang a solo, "The Last Mile of the Way." She had the high, smooth kind of voice you'd need for singing a child to sleep, but she was so shy she almost shut her eyes while she sang, with her head turned sideways like she was listening to something far off.

"Can't anybody preach Brother Dail's funeral," the preacher told us all. "Can't preach anybody's funeral, really. We're all preaching our own, by the way we live, and we're doing it every day. Doing it right now."

He started reading scripture that began, "Work for the night is coming . . ." and when he'd finished his sermon anybody who wanted to could stand up and say whatever they remembered of Emmett, and several did.

"He lived on some land I owned," one woman said, "and sometimes I'd go sit on the porch with him in the evening and we'd talk about different things over the country. He was good to people. He'd help you if he could."

"Emmett never bothered anybody," said another woman. "He kind of kept to himself. He wasn't one to say harm."

The pallbearers locked the casket lid down and carried it out while the piano played. The family followed just behind them down the aisle, and then everyone else went out, too.

There was hardly any crying at all, and nothing loud said. Emmett didn't like that sort of thing, when he was alive. While the casket was being loaded, the people who stood in the church yard talked about happy things: new babies, friends they'd seen lately, a good revival that was going on.

My grandfather showed me where the main road used to run, when he was a boy, beside a creek near the church. He said he'd walked that road many a time, at night, when he was courting my grandmother.

"I guess I'd known Emmett about as long as any friend I had," he said.

The day stayed sunny. No storm clouds. Good friends around. Quiet talk. The smell of good cooking coming from neighbors' houses.

As far as any of us knew, it was the kind of afternoon Emmett would have liked.

Willie Brasfield: The Tribute of No Tears

I was sad, of course. The particular kind of rocks-in-your-stomach sadness that comes with totally unchangeable things, like death.

I felt guilty, too.

Guilty that I was out early that springlike morning, running and running and running, feeling strong in my legs and clean in my lungs, and young, my heart pounding in my ears as the grass and dirt and sidewalks swooshed past in a blur of green beneath my jogging shoes.

Guilty that when I topped a certain hill I could almost see, across the treetops, the hospital where he was lying at that moment, where I'd gone to see him the day before, where he lay dying daily, hourly, by slow degrees under the dim and soundless fluorescent lights.

He was my great-uncle, but the "great" always went without saying; he was just Uncle Willie.

He was a barber for most of his life. He'd made enough money at it to buy some property and put some money in the bank. People joked him about being tight with a nickel.

And he had miraculously managed, for some seventy-odd years, never to spend a single day in a hospital. Until now.

On one of his worst days—a long stretch of hours spent staring at the hospital ceiling, too weary for his mouth to form a word—he noticed someone in the room reading a newspaper, and he raised his head and asked them to look on the financial page and see how much interest his money-market certificates were paying that week. They told him the percentage, and he nodded approvingly, weakly, and went back to staring at the ceiling again.

"That's him," was the only thing the members of the family could say, smiling, when they were told the story later. "That's Uncle Willie, all right."

And so there came to be yet another Uncle Willie legend, the last of hundreds.

He would rather pull somebody's leg than eat—and he really liked eating, mostly frog legs and pig knuckles and other things that made people draw up, squeamish, at the thought of it.

But he always kept plenty of good food on hand for visitors. If you came to his house, you ate. Something. That was understood.

He'd go to great lengths to pull a joke on somebody.

Like telling the paperboy that the man down the road (Willie's brother, my grandfather) was so bad about paying his debts that he'd better collect a month in advance before leaving any more papers.

Like telling a thirsty barbershop customer who inquired about the nearest bootlegger that there was one down the road a piece (Willie's brother, my grandfather, who is not only *not* a bootlegger but is a Sunday school superintendent to boot). "But you've got to be persistent," Uncle Willie cautioned the man, "because he doesn't sell to just anybody. He'll tell you, first off, that he doesn't know what you're talking about. Just keep on after him. Tell him you want the good stuff, and you know he's got it. Don't give up, and eventually he'll sell you some."

Stories, stories, and stories. More than one life's worth, it seems.

One night not too many weeks after his hospital stay I found myself walking slowly over a silent carpet, wearing an unaccustomed suit and tie, into a room overflowing with flowers and, at the middle of it, a silver-gray, satin-lined metal box.

I remember people in the crowd mentioning, as they walked past, that he didn't look like himself. Only when you got at one certain angle and looked close, he looked like himself, they decided, and they all showed each other the exact spot to stand so that he looked like himself, a little.

"It seems all wrong," his son-in-law said, shaking his head and barely smiling. "He looks like a diplomat or something."

I remember people in the crowd telling each other stories about him—outrageous things he'd done and said, jokes he'd pulled, jokes that had been pulled on him. It felt almost as if the night was just a regular gathering held in his honor and that he either had just left or hadn't arrived yet.

I remember that I surprised myself by not crying, not even once, and that the whole time I was there I didn't see anybody else cry, either.

And it came to me, then, the many ways that some special people who are dead don't really die. Because it was for certain he was still there, in all the room and all the people—in their tales and memories, if not in their very blood.

Everywhere, except the small gray satin-lined box.

6

A Thanksgiving Memory

A white-haired grandmother with red, stove-warmed cheeks sets the turkey at the head of the table for grandfather to carve.

The white curtain behind them is so full of sunshine it hurts the eyes. The silverware glistens, and the rows of people on both sides of the long table look to be almost bursting with the joy of it all.

The air is heavy with steam and the scent of baking.

Way down in the bottom corner of the picture, one guest looks up, away from the festive table, looks up at . . .

Me.

You've seen the picture, I know. Norman Rockwell painted it. It's called something like "Freedom from Want," and for half my life now it's been branded in my head as the chief icon of Thanksgiving.

I can't help it.

In my memory, Christmas is a confetti-like flurry of colors and smells and faces. So is Halloween. And the Fourth of July. Each is many things, a babel of memories, a blur. But not Thanksgiving.

Thanksgiving is that picture. Nothing more, nothing less.

How it got painted on my memory is something I've not told until now, though I've thought about it a lot lately.

It happened on a Thanksgiving eve, the year I turned thirteen. I figure if the statute of limitations hasn't run out by now, it never will.

So here goes:

Understand that I was not thirteen at just any old point in history.

Men were flying into space and John Kennedy reigned and the Beatles had just exploded into my $5 red plastic transistor radio and nothing was ever quite the same.

Teenagers were getting out of hand. When adults said the word "teenager," they said it in the half-angry, half-frightened tone one used when discussing derelicts or dangerous wounded animals.

We let our hair grow. We looked sullen, which took a lot of practice. We never said two words to an elder when one would do.

We were cool, and excited, and more than a little scared. We knew something big was in the works, that we were being set aside by history for some great work, such as saving the world.

We didn't know that the place we were slouching toward, like "some rough beast" in the famous poem, was the years of Woodstock and Vietnam.

All we knew was that something big was at stake and this was no time to stand on ceremony.

I had new wheels that year, too. A blue bicycle.

And I had specific instructions to go anywhere I wanted, on it, as long as I didn't cross over the Old Road west of our house and go into Bear Wallow Hollow (its real name, I swear).

That day-before-Thanksgiving afternoon, home from school, I unceremoniously pedaled to the edge of the Old Road, took a deep breath, and looked both ways to see that nobody was watching. Then . . .

Whooosh. I kept going, a streak of blue and chrome and spokes and shaggy hair, down into the forbidden hollow. I went up hills and down hills, over rock bluffs and through creeks into places so thick with underbrush the bike stalled and I had to get off and push, while the cold wind sang in my ears.

It's a new world, I reasoned (do thirteen-year-olds really reason, or are they just big hearts with feelings that change quicksilver-fast?), and it was about time all the old folks realized that this junk about tradition and family and don't-go-here, don't-go-there just wouldn't cut it anymore.

I walked and ran and rode and pushed and rode and walked some more, drunk on the cold air, until I came up against the face of a steep bluff and sat down to rest.

It began to get dark. And I realized, with the slow finality of a nightmare, that I had no idea which way home was.

I retraced my path, or tried to, but the trees and the hills had all changed places while my back was turned.

My stomach tightened. All the wind went out of me. It would have been very satisfying at that moment to have stretched out on the carpet of briars like a biblical character in sackcloth and ashes and wailed "Oh, woe is me!" loud enough to scare every raccoon on the Warrior River.

But I didn't. I ran, pushing my useless bicycle, hoping for some rock or hill to suddenly look familiar, to stand up and greet me and point the way back.

I remembered then that my grandmother—my grandparents lived next door— had been cooking, the last time I'd seen her. The windows of the kitchen were white with steam.

There was turkey and ham and a hen for the oven, dressing with onions, and a whole stove-top of stewing vegetables. I knew the cooking was still going on at that minute, would continue until the family arrived the next morning. My granddad would be cracking and sorting walnuts for cakes.

It was at some point in that darkening hour that the painting came to me, bright and real enough to touch: Norman Rockwell's big dining room, the red-cheeked woman, the glistening brown turkey.

I would have sold all my shares in the brave new world, at that minute, to have been sitting in that hot, steamy room cracking walnuts.

I plodded and circled and re-circled for what seemed like hours until finally, with the last few minutes of daylight, I climbed a bluff and found a broad, flat rock overhanging the valley that offered a clear view through the trees. And then I saw it:

The smoke from our chimneys, the gray haze it made lying gently across our roofs. They were tiny as doll houses, woven into the tapestry of green pine and red dirt: Our house and my grandparents' house and the Glovers' house and the Jones' house and the house where my great-grandmother had lived.

All there, all waiting. A couple of miles away. I saw the direction I needed to go, then—downhill, home.

It seems now that I flew there, though I know I must only have run, pushing the bicycle at speeds it had rarely achieved with me a-straddle it.

I remember stumbling in the dark, falling more than once; I remember limbs slapping my face, and I remember the way that I could speed up, dodging the limbs and snags from memory, when I reached familiar ground again.

I remember coming down the path to my grandparents' house, and sitting for several minutes on their back steps, gasping for breath and slapping my clothes free of dried mud and beggar-lice. I was thankful the windows were still so fogged no one saw me coming.

Breathing easier, finally, I walked into a kitchen so warm I could feel moisture condensing on my eyelashes.

And, wonder of wonders, nobody suspected a thing. Or, more probably, they did but just didn't let on.

Grandmother kept measuring, stirring, basting, testing the consistency of this or that with a fork, all the while humming an old church song. Granddad cracked walnuts and dozed from time to time. I sat down to help.

"Home" has been lots of places since then. Too many.

A college dormitory. An army barracks in Missouri. Various Southside apartments. And more.

But home will always be, for me, the view from the broad, flat rock in the orange-gray of dusk, the tapestry of woodsmoke and neighbors and kin.

And Thanksgiving will always be the suspended moment of the famous painting—the woman carrying the turkey and the man readying to carve it, the excited faces of the family, the white curtain full of sunshine.

I've learned only lately what purpose is served by the patient face of the man in the bottom corner of the frame, the face looking out of the picture toward me.

The face is telling me—telling us all, I think—that it knows where I've been and what I've done and that I'm loved anyway. It's telling me my chair is waiting, and that home is a place that is always downhill from wherever we are. Make a good start toward it, day or night, and you'll fly there.

Sit down, the patient face is telling me.

You're home.

7

Two Musicians

Reverend James Jackson: Radio as Pulpit

I've got the Holy Ghost . . . fie-yuh
Shut up in my bones . . . I said the Holy Ghost . . . fie-yuh
Shut up in my bones . . .

The music booms from the speakers on the wall of the small broadcasting studio, and it sounds so good to Reverend Theo Bailey that he can't sit still. He walks back and forth between the control panel and the turntable, clapping his hands high in the air and singing along.

It's a quarter till ten in the morning.

A door opens, and Reverend James E. Jackson sweeps through. He's a heavyset black man, middle forties, and his hat and coat are beaded with warm rain.

"Morning, Reverend," Bailey says, still hand-clapping, as Jackson lays down his briefcase and a small cardboard box he holds under his arm. "Listen to this part, listen . . ." says Bailey, pointing at the wall speaker. "Whoo-o-o-e-e-e, how about that?"

Jackson nods his approval and starts searching through shelves of albums for the ones he'll play on his 10:00 a.m. show. His foot taps lightly in time to the music.

Holy Ghost.. fie-yuh . . .

Shut up in my bones . . .

With a stack of albums ready, Jackson takes a set of headphones from the cardboard box and plugs himself into the console. When the clock says 10:00, he leans into the microphone and turns a knob to fade the music down.

"Good morning. This is the Radio Pastor Jackson, children," he intones, in a voice like chocolate syrup. "I'm here to lift you up! We got music from heaven, children, every day, here on WAGG. This next song goes out to Sister Woods, in Graysville—'I Need The Lord to Guide Me' . . ."

For the next four hours Jackson will preach, play records, exhort, chide, and inspire his listeners, pray for their ailments and their wayward children, advertise burial insurance, Lightning Loans, and rice, and give away free tickets to the Birmingham Stallions' games.

"To me, the radio's become another pulpit, five days a week," Jackson says, while the record plays. "It gives me a chance to keep my gospel sharpened so I can be ready on Sunday morning."

Come Sunday morning, Jackson, his wife Daisy, and their two children will get up before daylight and drive the 113 miles to the church he pastors, Mt. Zion Baptist in Columbus, Mississippi. The long-distance arrangement isn't a typical one, he admits.

"But you know, the Lord works in mysterious ways. I've been preaching for forty years," he says, and pauses a second to savor the puzzlement on a visitor's face. "I started when I was five," he explains with a grin.

"Anyhow, I've been preaching forty years and all of a sudden the joy of my salvation's becoming what it ought to be. It's a joy to me, getting up on Sunday to go preach."

The music fades out and he leans into the microphone as he cues another record.

"Take My Hand, Precious Lord," he says, as the singer echoes him.

Through the storm, through the night

Lead me on, to the light

Take my hand, precious Lord,

Lead me on . . .

"I tell you something, children—storms don't move the Lord. He rides on 'em. Yes, sir . . ."

Jackson removes his headset and takes a phone call off the air while the record plays. "You feelin' any better today, Reverend?" the caller asks. Yesterday, a Monday, Jackson was away sick.

"Much better, thank the Lord," the pastor says, his thumb keeping time to the music. "Had a touch of the flu. Sunday I got wet with sweat, preaching, and then got out in the cool air. I'll learn not to do that again. I tell you the truth, this is pneumonia weather . . ."

Jackson is the oldest of the daytime gospel station's four DJs. Other than the fact that he's gotten over his initial nervousness, his show hasn't changed much in the eight years since he started pastoring by radio, he says.

"Oh, I remember that first week. I wanted to do my best, but I didn't know what was going on. I'd start up un-cued records and no telling what all." He laughs and shakes his head. "It was.. .it was.. .total destruction."

But he and the audience survived. He still does the live call-in segment, "Prayer Time," every morning. And he still plays as much old-time gospel as he can.

Which is not to say there haven't been ups and downs. With its sister station, WENN-FM, doing well in the ratings with a playlist of contemporary soul music, the old WENN-AM changed its name to WAGG (which stands for "Alabama's Greatest Gospel" and, not coincidentally, for the initials of its owner, businessman A. G. Gaston) last year. WAGG radically changed its programming, as well.

The old-style church music was replaced with "contemporary Christian," a more Top 40 type of sound the station's management hoped would draw a larger share of young listeners.

The response was immediate—a storm of phone calls. But they weren't quite what the station had expected.

"Did we get calls?" Jackson repeats, and throws his head back with a rumbling laugh. "Lord, Lord, Lord . . ."

"People would say, 'Is this stuff what y'all gonna be playing?' and we'd say, 'Yes, it is,' and they'd say, 'Well, we ain't gonna listen, then . . .'"

The station's "contemporary" playlist was, to say the least, short-lived.

And Jackson doesn't seem at all displeased by the turn of events.

"I tell you," he says, "when you grow up listening to the great ones like Inez Andrews and Albertina Walker and Alex Bradford—he was from Bessemer, did you know that?—and the Pilgrim Jubilees and Mahalia Jackson, well . . . once you've heard them, you just don't want any of this new boom-bah-boom . . ."

When you're turning your radio dial to find WAGG, you notice it's just a gnat's breadth away from another AM gospel station, WCRT, whose audience is mainly white. But the two stations are as different as—no pun intended—light and dark.

WCRT's gospel is a soothing blend of orchestral arrangements, glistening violin sections, and conservatory-trained voices, mixed with a more upbeat "Jesus rock" that's reminiscent of the soft folk-rock of the 1960s.

Spin the dial a quarter-turn to WAGG, though, and you're met by foot stomping, hand clapping, tambourines, and rollicking rhythm-and-blues piano. There are voices that not only harmonize but also growl, groan, and moan, slide into a gruff lower register, and then ascend into an ecstatic squeal, sometimes making up new verses as they go.

Black gospel is a next-door neighbor to the blues. It's a kind of music that, like Reverend Jackson's preaching, works up a sweat.

Have you tried my Jesus?
Oh, let me tell you
Have you tried the King of Kings
In the lonely hours?
He's all right, yes he is
He's all right with me . . .

"I declare, he'll do it for you," Jackson is saying into the microphone. "Here's evangelist Shirley Caesar, 'Oh, How I Love Calling That Name' . . ."

"You see," Jackson says to his visitor, "that contemporary music just wasn't written for churches. It was written for the young folks. To give 'em that swing, you know?

"That new music's not . . ." His face strains mightily, searching for the right word. "It's not . . . conducive," he says. "It's not . . . edifying. I go to church to be edified. I don't allow my choir to do contemporary gospel.

"See, the gospel's the food I need to get me through the week. When I wake up in the morning, worried and burdened down, I don't need no contemporary. I need something to show me the way."

The clock is nearing eleven, the Prayer Time hour. Jackson checks his phone connections and begins a record by Katie Sanke, a slow and soulful version of "I Need Thee Every Hour."

(Unlike the younger DJs, who choose their music from a rack of convenient tape cartridges, Jackson patiently cues up each song the old way, from an album on a turntable. "Tape breaks," he explains. "Records don't.")

I need thee,
Yes I need thee
Every hour, dear Lord,
I need thee . . .

The phone lines all light up. "It's eleven o'clock, Birmingham, and it's Prayer Time," Jackson says softly. He punches a button on the phone.

"Good morning, Prayer Time . . ."

"Good morning, Reverend. How you?"

"Fine. You?"

"Pretty good, praise the Lord. I'm asking prayer for my brother, who's in the hospital. He'll be operated on tomorrow."

"All right."

"And keep on praying for me."

"We gonna do that, dahlin'. Thank you for calling. Good morning, Prayer Time . . ."

"How are you this morning, Reverend?"

"Good morning, Sister Clark. I'm fine."

Wo-o-oh-h, I need you, Lord
Just bless me . . .

The calls keep coming. They ask prayer for an elderly man in a nursing home, for a son who is drinking too much and "running with a bad crowd," for a brother in jail.

"Yeah, you get where you can recognize the voices," Jackson says later of the call-in segment. "Sometimes you can tell by the way a person sounds that they're not feeling well. They tell you all their problems. They become sort of a family to you. And if you go a while without hearing from them, you miss them and start trying to find out how they're doing.

"In our churches, see, a pastor is more than just their preacher. He's their instructor, their big brother, their playmate. People lean on their pastor. They depend on him. When my young people mess up in school, I'm the first to know. They come talk to me about it. And when folks decide to marry, they come to me for counseling."

Most announcers dread handling live phone calls because of pranksters or obscene talkers, but Jackson says he's never used a tape delay system. "Oh, sometimes a caller will talk a bunch of bull, but I know how to handle 'em. I shame 'em out of it. I tell 'em how dangerous it is to play with the Lord. Old Belshazar, in the Bible, found that out. Yes, sir. Belshazar paid the consequences."

I need thee, Lord,
I need thee . . .

The call-ins have ended; it's time for Jackson's daily prayer. He leans across the studio console, holds its edges like he would a pulpit, closes his eyes tightly, and begins:

"God, our father, we're thankful we can come to you. We can come as we are, wearied and wounded and sad. We can come broken, we can come healthy, we can come ill, and you always have time to listen to your children's cry."

Behind Jackson, a large plate-glass window shows the adjoining WENN studio, where young announcers come and go to the incongruous beat of unheard dance music, wearing bright sweatshirts and lots of gold jewelry.

". . . And God, we thank you for enabling us to make the journey through last night. That while we were yet so close to death, you would not allow death to cross the line, but bidded these golden moments to roll on a little while longer. And this morning we come, just to have this little talk with you. Because we're strengthened whenever we take the time out to connect into your powerhouse."

The prayer gradually grows louder, as Katie Sanke still sings low in the background. Some of Jackson's words turn into musical notes, and he punctuates phrases by striking the console with his hand.

Then he comes to "Amen," and reaches behind him to begin playing another record.

He's using my hands

To do his will . . .

The pastor spins around on his stool and stretches his legs. Through the plate glass, a young announcer and a girlfriend are play-wrestling over a magazine. They look up and see Jackson. He smiles and nods at them, sighing to himself.

The Radio Pastor has two and a half hours to go. The rain is coming down harder outside. He searches his coat pockets for his medicine.

Look at these old feet of mine

Climbing over rocky hills . . .

Jackson flips a switch on the console to play an hourly news update, and then goes over to look through the shelves of albums.

"Even when I'm feeling down, I try to do a show that's uplifting, you know? When you get older, your concept of life is different.

"I'm taking guitar lessons, did I tell you? Bought me an electric guitar. Got a good price on it." He grins broadly. "Yessir, I want to be the best guitar player in the city of Birmingham."

He cues up the new album, while tapping his foot to the one that's already playing. The rain is coming down harder still.

Jackson looks up. "The Lord said be faithful and he'd give me a crown of life. So what have I got to worry about, huh?"

Bobby Horton: Troubadour of the Confederacy

The stage is dark. Then from behind the curtain comes a flickering orange light, and a man in a gray Confederate soldier's uniform walks out, carrying a kerosene lantern and a battered banjo.

The Civil War has just started, he tells the crowd, and spirits are running high. After all, it's common knowledge that one Southerner can whip ten

Yankees, so the war should be over in a matter of weeks. If you want to get in on the fighting, you'd better hurry.

He sets down the lantern, straps on his banjo, and starts playing a sprightly dance tune:

If you want to have a good time
Jine the cavalry,
Jine the cavalry,
Jine the cavalry.
If you want to catch the devil
If you want to have fun
If you want to smell hell
Jine the cavalry . . .

Before the evening is over, Bobby Horton will have talked and sung his way through all four years of the long-ago war—the victories, defeats, atrocities, and suffering on both sides, and the eventual destruction of the entire Southern way of life.

A former accountant for a life insurance company, Horton has toured the U.S. and Canada for more than ten years with the Birmingham-based folk and Bluegrass group Three on a String. But during the past few years, his Civil War songs—a project that began as a one-time program for a local historical group—have expanded to fill four solo albums and a series of concerts that climaxed this spring when the National Park Service invited him to perform at a gathering in Vicksburg, Mississippi, commemorating the 125th anniversary of the decisive battle.

In 1961, when Horton was ten years old, his family visited the memorial park at Chicamauga, Georgia, during the Civil War Centennial. "Somehow a light just turned on in my head," he remembers. "I've been fascinated by the war ever since."

And he isn't alone. The sheer volume of information available to an enthusiast is almost impossible for the uninitiated to imagine. Nearly 60,000 books on the topic are in the Library of Congress alone—more than on any other subject except the Bible—not counting the thousands of unpublished manuscripts and memoirs written by men and women who survived the war years. At least nine national monthly magazines are devoted entirely to articles about the war, and groups around the country meet regularly by the hundreds to re-enact Civil War battles, with authentic uniforms and weapons.

Why the endless obsession with four short years of distant history? Partly the magnitude of the suffering: more Americans died in the Civil War than in World War I, World War II, and Vietnam combined. And most of the returning soldiers were maimed in some way—losing a finger, a hand, an eye, an arm or leg.

But more than numbers, the war abounds in dramatic ironies that even the greatest of scriptwriters couldn't have invented. Thinking of the conflict as simply a war between North and South overlooks the fact that men from every state fought on both sides.

The political questions that precipitated the war—many of which had nothing to do with slavery, but rather states' rights and economics—bitterly divided thousands of families, pitting brother against brother, father against son, uncle against nephew. Even three of Mary Todd Lincoln's brothers died fighting on the side of the Confederacy.

When the Birmingham chapter of Sons of Confederate Veterans—of which Horton is a member—asked him to put together a program of Civil War music for one of their meetings, he went to the downtown library's Southern History Room to do his research. He hoped to find a few dozen songs to choose from. But what he found astonished him—and the librarians who helped him, as well. In the Tutwiler Collection of Southern Life they uncovered more than 700 songs, many of them the actual sheet music published in the 1860s. "It was a gold mine," he remembers. "It was unbelievable."

After his presentation to the Veterans' group, Horton felt "sort of a letdown" because he'd only been able to scratch the surface of the period's music. In his spare time he started recording some of the songs on a small multi-track recorder in his kitchen, "just as keepsakes," singing the harmonies and playing all the instruments himself: banjo, guitar, mandolin, trumpet, fife, dulcimer, fiddle, and drum.

Eventually he accumulated enough material for an album and, with the help of friend Brant Beene, mixed it onto a cassette tape he called "Homespun Songs of the Confederate States of America," and promoted it with some ads in Civil War publications. National Public Radio started including his songs on its syndicated series *Folk Sampler*.

It wasn't long until he received a glowing letter from a historical group wanting to book him for its convention and distribute his album to their members. But when he looked into the offer, he discovered that the organization was affiliated with the Ku Klux Klan.

"I was depressed for days," he says. "I figured, well, if what I'm doing is going to be that misunderstood, then forget it. I quit." It was only after long talks with some good friends that he became convinced not to abandon his collecting and recording.

In a time when the nightly news carries video footage of attempts to tear the Confederate flag off the capitol building in Montgomery, finding the right audience for the music of the Confederacy (three of his albums contain various arrangements of "Dixie") has been somewhat of a battle in itself.

"I really despise the fact that groups like the Klan have taken the Confederate flag and disgraced it by making it a symbol of racism," Horton says. "That's not the way it is at all."

It's late at night and he's sitting in the kitchen with his shoes off, his sock feet drawn up in the chair. An orange-colored cat walks noiselessly beside the countertop where Horton's recording equipment sits. A Confederate flag is tacked high on the wall. Through the door, long shelves of history books can be seen in the lamplight of the den.

"My son's black friends don't think anything about the flag being there. They know me. They know what I believe. But everything has gotten so whitewashed these days in the history books . . . you really have to search for the truth. Our kids are being taught little facets of what went on, but they never really get the big picture.

"Sure, slavery was wrong. And a lot of people in the South knew, deep down, that it was wrong. But only a tiny minority of Southerners owned slaves. To the working man—the ordinary, common man, not the big land-owners—slavery was basically a very unpopular subject. Not so much from a moral point of view, but from the fact that slaves took jobs away from poor people.

"The war wasn't fought to free the slaves. At least it didn't start out that way. We would never have gone to war over slavery alone. Even when President Lincoln signed the Emancipation Proclamation, it only freed the slaves in the *Southern* states, not the slaves in the border states that were still loyal to the Union. Lincoln needed those states' support. He couldn't afford to antagonize them.

"Some experts say that in another generation slavery would most likely have died out, anyway. The war was started by wealthy people, by powerful business interests, like shipping. And the poor common man, the one who had to do the actual fighting, was caught in the middle. Isn't that the way it always goes?

"I have ancestors who fought for the Confederacy and ancestors who fought for the Union. If you look closely, you find a lot that was right and a lot that was wrong on both sides. Of course, I don't read history without bias. Nobody does. And I'm sure if I were black and I'd grown up seeing these hate groups use the Confederate flag, I'd hate it too.

"But there were a lot of honorable men, back in the war, who sacrified everything they had for what they believed in. It was a simpler time. It was a time when, if a man felt something strongly, he stood up for it. Pride was everything, back then. That's my birthright, and nobody can take that away. Our ancestors are getting a bad rap in a lot of ways, and they're not around to defend themselves, and that hurts me."

One of Horton's fondest memories is the night a young black woman came up to him after one of Civil War concerts, shook his hand, and told him that his music made her proud to be an American.

In the same audience that night was Mary Bess Paluzzi, one of the librarians who had helped Horton find the treasure trove of old sheet music:

"When somebody who grew up black in Birmingham during the 1960s can feel that way about the music of the Confederacy," Paluzzi says, "I think it's a testament to how powerful those songs are. But it also says something about Bobby as a performer, and as a person.

"He talks you through the war chronologically. You feel the fervor of those early months, the confidence they had. And then you see the slow deterioration as men start longing for their wives, their shoes are wearing out, food gets harder to find. They're getting so tired, and every day they watch their friends falling dead around them. You see the whole war through the eyes of the common soldier."

When o'er the desert through burning rays
With a heavy heart I tread
Or when I breast the cannon's blaze
And be mourned by comrades dear

Then, oh then, I will think of home and you
And our flag shall kiss the wind
With huzzahs for our cause and our Southland too
And the girls we leave behind

Then adieu, then adieu, 'tis the last bugle strain
That is falling on the ear
Should it be so decreed that we ne'er meet again
Oh, remember the young volunteer . . .
—from "The Young Volunteer," by John H. Hewitt

No two of Horton's concerts are the same. He doesn't use a script or a song list, but prefers to improvise as he goes. It's riskier that way, he admits, "but you also get that big rush of adrenaline that comes from not knowing what's going to happen next."

The banjo he plays on stage is his grandfather's; it was manufactured in 1881. The trumpet he uses was carried through the war by a Union cavalryman.

The surprising thing about the Civil War songs is that in Horton's treatment they don't come off—as so much "historic" music does—as either dry museum pieces or as tongue-in-cheek fun poked at people of a more backward era.

He doesn't so much sing the songs as *inhabit* them. Partway through a performance, people in the audience often look around in a kind of trance, as if to reassure themselves by each other's presence that the year is really 1988.

"Robert E. Lee always claimed that you couldn't have an army without music," Horton says. "It's hard for us, with our radios and Walkmans and compact discs and VCRs, to imagine how much music meant to people back in those days. It was their only form of entertainment. And there weren't any recordings, so the only way you could have music was to make it yourself.

"Armies always went into a big fight with music playing. In one instance I know of, a regiment's drummer, who was leading them, was killed just as they were starting to advance. So they found a soldier who had a fiddle in his knapsack, and he got out front and fiddled them into battle." Horton's wife, Lynda, had a great-great-uncle who was drummer for a Union regiment.

It's estimated that more than 10,000 songs were written during the Civil War. The urge to make music was so irrepressible that soldiers on guard duty often had to be punished for breaking into song.

"Every war inspires its own distinctive music," says Bob Housch of the National Park Service, which sells Horton's albums in the gift shops of all its Civil War memorial parks. "But the Civil War is special because both sides spoke the same language. So you have a great deal of 'crossover' music, Southern songs that became popular in the North and vice versa. And it was common to have several different versions of a song, all with the same tune.

"A lot of Civil War music was recorded in the 1960s and 70s, but much of it was either done in sort of a 'hippie' style or was backed up with a full symphony orchestra. In both cases, the flavor of the original music was lost completely. But Bobby's tapes are outselling all others at our parks now. His real achievement, I think, is that he's made the music simple again, so simple that it's . . . well, *elegant* is the best word."

"What's amazing," Horton says, "is not just that there were so *many* songs written back then, but that there were so many *good* songs. Any number of them have melodies so striking that if they came out today they could be on a radio station's Top 40."

Jeb Stuart, the South's audacious and controversial cavalry genius, had the reputation of being the greatest music lover of the Confederacy. "Jine the Cavalry" was his theme song, and at night in the camps he'd often get together a quartet around the fire to sing hymns and ballads.

When Stuart lay dying from a gunshot wound to his stomach, he asked the soldiers standing around his bed to sing "Rock of Ages" with him. He tried hard to sing the bass part, but he was shot so badly he couldn't take in enough air to hold a note. A minute later he was dead.

"Rock of Ages," on Horton's second album, is dedicated to Jeb Stuart. And the hymn "On Jordan's Stormy Banks" is in memory of Sam Davis, a Tennessee teenager who, about to be hanged as a spy, was offered a pardon if he'd tell who had given him the information. "I cannot betray the trust of a friend," the boy is reported to have said, and as the rope was being placed around his neck he asked the people in the crowd to sing "On Jordan's Stormy Banks."

On Jordan's stormy banks I stand
And cast a wishful eye
To that fair land of joy and love
Where my possessions lie . . .

The mounting casualties of the first full year of war took everyone by surprise. It was a far cry from the weeks of pre-war excitement, when men who were hesitant to enlist in the cause would find anonymous packages on their doorsteps containing petticoats. One Congressman sarcastically offered the use of his handkerchief "to wipe up all the blood that would be spilled" in the brief skirmish he predicted would follow.

The war had initially been viewed by both sides as something of a summertime lark. The first major engagement at Manassas, twenty-five miles south of Washington, D.C., actually had to be delayed so that onlookers with picnic baskets could be persuaded to move out of the Union army's path. But by sundown 1,200 men were dead and more than 3,000 wounded—the costliest single battle in American history up until that time. The South routed the north decisively, and gained a false sense of confidence that obscured the ominousness of the casualty figures. In coming months, troops would often see more deaths in a single hour of battle than happened in the entire War of Independence.

It was the foot soldiers of the Civil war who invented "dog tags." A regiment would often lose 25 percent of its men in a battle. At Gettysburg and other major engagements the figure was more than 80 percent. Knowing how likely they were to die, soldiers began lettering their names and addresses on their handkerchiefs and pinning them to their uniforms before walking into battle.

Historians call the Civil War the first "modern" war because of the many technological innovations of the day. Probably the most significant was the breech-loading rifle, which could fire seven shots to the old musket's one and was so much deadlier at long range that it made all former wisdom about infantry fighting obsolete. It was also the first war to use the telegraph, balloon observation, trench fighting, wire entanglements, and armored ships.

And it was the first war to be thoroughly documented by photographs. Some 75 percent of them were made with 3-D stereo cameras. The resulting pictures, seen through Viewmaster-like "stereopticons" that had been popularized for viewing photos of nature scenics, suddenly brought piles of rotting corpses into the country's living rooms—in stark contrast to the more genteel propaganda accounts of battles carried by newspapers and magazines. The effect was comparable to the unremitting television coverage, in the 1970s, of the war in Southeast Asia.

There are other striking parallels to America's experience in Vietnam. "In the beginning," Horton says, "one side would do *this* small thing, and the other side would do *that* small thing—you know, 'no big deal'—back and forth, back and forth, until one day both sides wake up and realize, my God, what have we done?"

If the war had been decided by resources alone, the South would have been beaten almost immediately. The North had more than double the population of the South, four times as much money in the bank, almost triple the mileage of railroads, and—a crucial statistic—nearly *six* times the number of factories. It was the drastically different needs of the North's industrial economy and the South's agricultural economy that had stoked the constant legislative squabbling that led to the war.

The South, though, had two big advantages that made the contest less lopsided—it was fighting on its own soil and, at least in the beginning, had far better military officers. West Point-trained Robert E. Lee was held in such awe by Lincoln that, when war looked imminent, he immediately offered him command of the Union army. Lee, a Virginia native, refused. He could not, he told Lincoln, "take up my sword against the land of my birth."

A great tragedy that prolonged the war, one historian has said, was that the opposing forces were often so evenly matched. As he put it, "When they met they could bang the hell out of each other, killing men by the thousands, but neither side could quite manage to disable the other completely."

As the contest wore on, the Union erected a naval blockade to cut off the South's source of supplies. Railroads were dug up, fields burned. The deprivation that resulted left few Southern families untouched. Formerly wealthy matrons had to make dresses out of curtains and coats out of old carpet. Troops hemmed in for weeks during the siege of Vicksburg lived in caves and cooked their mules for meat. When the supply of mules ran out, they caught and ate rats.

"Making do" under horrible conditions was a great point of pride in the Confederacy, and many of the songs during the closing years of the war were about the sacrifices they made for their cause. One of the most popular was "The Homespun Dress":

Oh yes, she is a Southern girl
And glory in the name
And boasted with far greater pride
Than glittering wealth or fame

She envies not the Northern girl
Her robes of beauty rare,
Though diamonds grace her snowy neck
And pearls bedeck her hair

So hurrah, hurrah
For the sunny South so dear
Three cheers for the homespun dress
That Southern ladies wear . . .

The song also inspired the name of Horton's music label, Homespun Records. On the kitchen table beside him is a stack of mail, most of it orders for his albums. The return addresses are from Baltimore, Maryland; Fredonia, New York; Mesa, Arizona; Ocala, Florida; Fairfield, Virginia;

Chicago, Illinois; and Green Mile, Texas. One order comes from France.

Many of the orders include a personal note telling about an ancestor's Civil War experiences. "Every family has its stories," Horton says, "and they feel compelled to tell them, even to a stranger." He's accumulated hundreds of histories through the mail over the years.

One of the most haunting was from a family in South Carolina whose great-grandmother was tortured and raped by drunken Union troops in the waning days of the war. Her oldest son had been killed in the fighting two weeks earlier and was buried in a pasture behind the house. One of the Union soldiers dug up the corpse and brought it into the house to "watch."

In the struggling, one of the men accidentally knocked over a lantern and set the house afire. All the soldiers but one escaped. When the war ended the family left the soldier's skeleton in the ruin of the house, where it remained until recently, bleached by the sun and rain, a constant reminder of the war years. "For most of my life," the man wrote, "I could see his bones from my kitchen window."

Then, recently, the family got a letter from one of the burned soldier's descendants, who had tracked down the whereabouts of the body. They were coming to South Carolina, they said, to give him a military funeral at the site and bring the skeleton home for burial. "When they arrived," the man wrote Horton, "we handed them the bones in a plastic garbage bag and told them to get off our land."

"So the war's not over," Horton says. "I mean, technically it is. But in ways, it's not. Maybe it will be, someday."

Three hundred thousand Yankees
Is stiff in Southern dust
We got three hundred thousand
Before they conquered us

They died of Southern fever
And Southern steel and shot
I wish they was three million
Instead of what we got

I can't take up my musket
And fight 'em now no more
But I ain't gonna love 'em,
Now that is certain sure

And I don't want no pardon
For what I was and am
I won't be reconstructed
And I don't care a damn . . .

—from "Oh, I'm a Good Old Rebel"

Horton sits on his living room floor with the remote control of the video recorder in his hand. On the television screen, black-and-white portraits of Civil War soldiers dissolve from one to another. The faces look alternately proud, angry, numb, resigned, horrified. As they pass, Horton tells about each one.

"That one is from Georgia . . . he's from Tennessee . . . he's from Louisiana, see the costume?"

One picture shows a frail, frightened boy holding a bugle. "That one is fourteen years old. Look at those eyes. He died the day after the picture was taken. At Shiloh."

The videotape is from the documentary series "The Divided Union" that aired last fall on the Arts and Entertainment Network. The music under the closing photographs—a chilling, ethereal arrangement of "Dixie" played on harp, oboe, and orchestral bells—was borrowed by the producers of the series from Horton's third album. He did the arrangement after coming home from a visit to Shiloh, where he stood in the burial trenches and was shown how the Confederate corpses were stacked. "I had to write something really emotional to deal with how I was feeling," he says.

One of the ironies of history is that the much-maligned "Dixie" was one of Abraham Lincoln's favorite songs. From time to time he asked Union military bands to play it for him, commenting to them, "It's got the catchiest tune I ever heard."

Horton says people often ask him why the Civil War inspires such a depth of feeling in Americans who are several generations removed from it, why so many historians around the world devote their entire careers to studying it.

"One winter," he says, "Let's see . . . it would have been December of 1864, at the Battle of Nashville. It came an awful blizzard. The ground was solid ice.

"There were thousands of Southern men out there fighting, with the ground all iced over and most of them . . ." He swallows hard. "Most of them didn't even have *shoes* . . ." He looks away for a second, out the darkened window, as if there's something there to see. The edges of his eyes glisten, suddenly moist. He takes a deep breath and goes on.

"Depending on how you look at it, what they were doing was either very stupid . . . or very, very admirable. You talk about dedication. Talk about pride . . ."

He shrugs, sits back against the couch. "These people were real," he says. "They're not just something in a book. They're real. They lived.

"I have Union ancestors, a family from New York. I know they fought for the North out of a sense of duty and honor, and I'm proud of them. I have an affection for the Union soldier, for the common man.

"And when it comes down to it, I have to admit that the war turned out the way it should have. That things are as they should be.

"But, yeah, I lean to the South. It's my birthright. I always will."

About the Author

Dale Short, a native of Shanghi, Alabama, has worked as a writer, editor, teacher, advertising photographer, and audiovisual producer. His fiction and journalism have appeared in *Newsweek, The New York Times, USA Today, American Lawyer, The Runner, Country Music, Redbook, National Observer, Appalachian Journal, Southern Exposure, Roanoke Review, South Carolina Review, Birmingham, Detroit, Aura,* and other periodicals, and he was selected as the outstanding young writer in America in a contest sponsored by *Redbook*. His childhood in Shanghi was the basis for his radio drama *Evening Glass*, produced by WBHM and broadcast by public radio affiliates, and for *A Mountain Chord*, a collection of one-act plays produced by Berea College in Kentucky. He was host for two years of *Saturday Afternoon on the Front Porch*, a weekly radio show on Birmingham's WVSU-FM featuring Bluegrass and old-time gospel music, and for seventeen years taught photojournalism at the University of Alabama at Birmingham and fiction and playwriting at the Alabama School of Fine Arts. He lives in Jasper, where he works as a grandfather, journalist, and video producer. His weekly columns still appear in the *Daily Mountain Eagle*, and he's the host of the radio show "Music from Home" on WJLX-FM, which is archived on his web page, carrolldaleshort.com.

www.ingramcontent.com/pod-product-compliance
Lightning Source LLC
Chambersburg PA
CBHW031305060726
47590CB00003B/1075

* 9 7 8 1 6 0 3 0 6 2 0 7 7 *